55 EMBROIDERY ✷ PROJECTS ✷ IN MINIATURE

55 EMBROIDERY �֎ PROJECTS �֎ IN MINIATURE

Meg Evans

BCA

LONDON   NEW YORK   SYDNEY   TORONTO

This book is dedicated to the memory of my mother,
who enjoyed the pleasure of her embroidery into her ninety-second year

Spring in the Garden

*(Page 2) A selection of embroidered boxes including three nesting boxes, fitted
circular box, hat-shaped box, pulled-work box pincushion, gold initial box
and dressing table box*

*(Page 6) The many different projects featured in the book include miniature
pictures, carrier bag, circular basket, miniature furniture and carpets in
$^{1}/_{12}$ scale and pulled-fabric pictures*

Photography by Di Lewis

This edition published 1994 by BCA by arrangement with
David & Charles

CN 3046

Copyright © text and designs Meg Evans 1994
Photographs David & Charles 1994
First published 1994

Typeset by ABM Typographics Ltd, Hull
and printed in Great Britain
by Butler & Tanner Ltd, Frome
for David & Charles
Brunel House   Newton Abbot   Devon

Contents

Introduction

THROUGHOUT the ages people have derived pleasure from creating beautiful things for daily use. Carpets, cushions, saddle cloths, tents, sails and clothing were often beautifully embroidered, demonstrating the creativity of their makers. Many of today's designs are taken from historical embroidery, and from a range of other sources such as architecture and old design books. When worked on traditional fabrics, such embroidery is relaxing and satisfying.

In this book I have set out to show how traditional techniques and modern materials can be used together to create a range of interesting designs for small projects that are both useful and decorative.

Plastic canvas has been available for a decade or more. Originally sold only in 7-bar mesh (7 bars to the inch), it was first used for easily-made, mass appeal items, which lacked finesse and style. It was also popular as a children's teaching aid and for elderly embroiderers with failing sight.

Some embroiderers may have reservations about the use of plastic canvas but, in my view, since it is completely covered by the embroidery and therefore not seen, these are misplaced. Plastic canvas has many advantages; it is easy to handle and will not go out of shape, it is rigid and therefore ideal for constructed items such as boxes, and it is washable. However, it does lack the suppleness of cotton canvas, and the finest gauge available (14-bar mesh) is not very strong. Plastic canvas will never replace cotton canvas, but in appropriate situations it is unbeatable. (See Chapter 11 for more details on plastic canvas.)

The projects in this book use both traditional materials and plastic canvas. Some, such as the canvas work and pulled-work pincushions and needlecases, are completely traditional. Others, like the bags and baskets in Chapter 1, are on plastic canvas only. In others I have used combinations of embroidery on natural fabrics, embroidery on plastic canvas, and plastic canvas covered by fabric, to achieve the desired effect.

The range of possibilities is enormous – and I have written this book to encourage others to begin experimenting with the old and the new. I hope you find the process as enjoyable as I have! Please note that it is advisable to read Chapter 11, which explains the techniques and basic methods used throughout the book, before starting any of the projects.

– 1 –
Bags and Baskets

*T*HESE small bags and baskets are quick to make and they may be used in a great variety of ways. You can fill them with flowers, Easter eggs or special small gifts – or delight the heart of any small girl with a hat-shaped box for her special treasures.

The baskets would make attractive table decorations for a special occasion. For a wedding, they could be stitched in colours to tone with the bridesmaids' dresses, and filled with flowers to match the bride's bouquet. The bridegroom's present to the bridesmaids, if small enough, could be presented in the hat box, with the ribbon made from the same material as their dresses.

For a Christening, the dainty cradle would make a delightful table decoration, stitched in pink or blue with matching embroidered bed linen.

The bag and basket designs detailed here are just a few suggestions – let your imagination get to work, and make them in any size or colour you wish.

Large and small circular baskets, cradle, hat boxes and carrier bag

Carrier Bag

A miniature carrier, like a doll's shopping bag, seems to have universal appeal. It is the perfect size for presenting a small but special gift such as jewellery or a lace handkerchief.

This little bag is worked using 10-bar plastic canvas. If a larger bag is preferred, using 7-bar canvas instead of 10-bar would more than double the capacity. The border could be made wider by increasing the number of rows of tent stitch, or by adding one in double cross stitch. The inner cream area, or the size of the leaves, could be enlarged. Remember that the central flower is the focal point of the design, and you should aim to keep a balance between the two sections.

Carrier bag

⁄⁄⁄⁄	blue	
⊠⊠⊠⊠	dark pink	
‖‖‖‖	light pink	
▲▲▲▲	green	
· · · ·	cream	

MATERIALS

10 x 5in (250 x 125mm) plastic canvas, 10 bars
    per inch (25mm)
Anchor Pearl Cotton No 5
    two skeins: 161 blue
    one skein each of: 73 light pink; 75 dark pink;
    216 green
Paterna Stranded Wool (Yarn)
    two skeins: 263 cream

From the plastic canvas, cut two sides 33 x 31
bars, two gussets 33 x 14 bars, one base 31 x 14
bars and two handles 42 x 3 bars.
    Use pearl cotton singly for the cross stitch,
doubled for the tent stitch and overcasting. Use
a single strand of cream wool (yarn) for the

cross stitch. Work the central patterned area in
cross stitch. Tent stitch is used elsewhere.

HANDLES

Leaving the first and last four bars of canvas uncovered, work a single line of tent stitch down
the centre in light pink. Overcast the edges
beside the stitching in blue. Tack (baste) the
handles behind the upper edge of each side
piece, underlapping by four bars and making
sure that the handles are evenly spaced.

FIG 1 Stitch diagram for handles

SIDES AND BASE

For the sides, work the embroidery following the chart, taking the stitches through the handles at the same time. Start with the top row of blue pearl cotton to anchor the handles in place. Embroider the base following the chart.

GUSSETS

Embroider the gussets, leaving the centre two bars uncovered as shown. Carefully cut between the two uncovered bars, leaving the last bar uncut. Trim off the spikes. Fold gusset in half lengthways, with right sides inside and edges matched up and, starting at the lower end, overcast to join. For extra strength, work to the top of the gusset and down again.

TO MAKE UP THE BAG

Place the lower edge of one side against the base, with edges matching and wrong sides facing. Overcast together using blue pearl. Join the

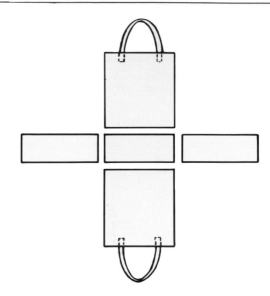

FIG 2 Making up a carrier bag

gussets and the other side in the same way. Join the corners and overcast the top edge, taking the stitching through the handles as you work.

Circular Basket

This decorative basket could be used for presents or sweets, or filled with flowers. For Easter, it could be stitched in yellows and greens and decorated with fresh flowers or Easter eggs.

The basket is lined with a second piece of plastic canvas, which gives extra stability and ensures a neat finish. The size of the basket may be varied by using any of the pre-formed plastic-canvas circles.

LARGE BASKET

MATERIALS

14 x 6in (355 x 150mm) plastic canvas, 10 bars per inch (25mm)
4¼in (106mm) diameter plastic-canvas circle
Paterna Stranded Wool (Yarn)
    four skeins: 263 cream
Anchor Pearl Cotton No 5
    one skein each of: 161 blue; 76 dark pink; 73 light pink; 216 green

From the plastic canvas, cut one side 135 x 18 bars, one lining 130 x 17 bars, one backing strip 8 x 18 bars, one backing strip 8 x 17 bars and one handle 96 x 8 bars.

Use the pearl cotton singly for the cross and edge stitch, doubled for the tent stitch and overcasting. Use a single strand of wool (yarn) for the cross stitch, three strands for the satin stitch.

Large and small circular baskets

HANDLE

Leaving four bars of the plastic canvas un-covered at each end, work cross stitch as shown in the chart. Edge stitch beside the embroidery in blue.

SIDE

Tack (baste) the (8 x 18) backing strip to the right short edge of the side piece so that it underlaps by four bars. Following the chart, embroider the side piece leaving four bars un-covered at each end. Lap the left-hand edge over the backing strip to join into a ring and com-plete the embroidery through both layers.

FIG 3 Backing strip to side

FIG 4 Joining into a ring

BASE

Work rounds of satin stitch, covering the cent-ral intersection with a cross stitch.

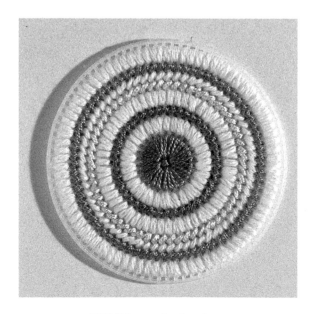

FIG 5 Large basket base

LINING

Mark the centre of the lining piece with a knot. With the wrong side of the handle facing the lin-ing, tack (baste) the handle in place, underlapping by four bars, four bars to the left of the marked centre. Tack (baste) the 8 x 17 backing strip to the right short edge, underlapping it by four bars. Leaving four bars uncovered at the left short edge, work sloping lines of small diamond stitch to within about 1½in (40mm) of the right edge.

Tack (baste) the left hand edge over the backing strip, right side inside, to form a ring. Tack (baste) the free end of the handle beside the backing strip, underlapping it by the four uncovered bars. Com-plete the embroidery through both layers. Over-cast round the lower edge.

FIGS 6 and 7 Basket into ring and Stitching up basket

TO MAKE UP THE BASKET

Place the side over the base and overcast all round to join, in blue. As the base piece has larger holes than the side, stitch twice into the same hole of the base where necessary. Place the lining inside and edge stitch all round the upper edge to join the two layers, taking the stitches through the handle at the same time.

(above) Large basket   (below) Small basket

SMALL BASKET

MATERIALS

10 x 4½in (250 x 113mm) plastic canvas, 10 bars
   per inch (25mm)
3in (75mm) diameter plastic-canvas circle
Paterna Stranded Wool (Yarn)
   three skeins: 263 cream
Anchor Pearl Cotton No 5
   one skein each of: 161 blue; 975 light blue;
   216 green

From the plastic canvas, cut one side 90 x 13
bars, one lining 86 x 12 bars, one backing strip
8 x 13 bars and one 8 x 12 bars and one handle
64 x 6 bars.

   Proceed as for the large basket, following the
chart above.

The Hat Box

This little hat-shaped box is made in two parts. The inner crown is attached to a circle for the base, and the outer crown fits on top.

The instructions and materials are given for making the medium-sized hat, and the materials are given for smaller and larger sizes.

Plastic-canvas circles are available in standard sizes up to 12in (300mm) diameter, but any size could be cut.

MEDIUM HAT

MATERIALS

10 x 3in (250 x 75mm) plastic canvas, 7 bars per inch (25mm)

10 x 1in (250 x 25mm) plastic canvas, 10 bars per inch (25mm)

4¼in (106mm) and 3in (75mm) diameter plastic-canvas circles

Paterna Stranded Wool (Yarn)
  three skeins: 263 cream

Anchor Pearl Cotton No 5
  one skein: 161 blue
  small quantities of: 216 green; 76 dark pink; 74 light pink

From the 7-bar plastic canvas, cut one side 65 x 8 bars and one inner crown 60 x 7 bars. From the 10-bar plastic canvas, cut one band 98 x 8 bars.

Use three strands of wool (yarn) throughout. Use pearl cotton singly for the cross stitch, doubled for the overcasting.

SIDES

Leaving four bars of canvas uncovered at each short edge of the side piece (65 x 8), work rows of brick stitch over two bars in cream wool (yarn). Overlap the short edges, matching up the bars, and complete the embroidery through both layers, so forming a ring. Slip the needle under the last bar and overcast the edge to neaten. Repeat for the inner crown. Overcast along one edge on each piece.

CIRCLES

Work in rounds of satin and tent stitch as shown in Fig 5, leaving the sixth bar from the edge uncovered on the larger circle. The inner crown will be stitched along this line. Work a cross stitch over the centre intersection.

BAND

Leaving the first and last four bars uncovered, work rows of cross stitch following the chart on page 15 for the large basket handle. Overlap the ends and complete the embroidery through both layers. Overcast both edges in blue.

TO MAKE UP THE HAT BOX

Place the smaller circle in position over the uncovered edge of the side section, and overcast all round to join. Place the inner crown over the larger circle, uncovered bars matched up, and overcast to join them. Slip the band into place.

FIG 8 Side to top

FIG 9 Crown to base

Large, medium and small hat boxes and cradle

LARGE HAT

MATERIALS

12 x 3in (300 x 75mm) plastic canvas, 7 bars per
   inch (25mm)
5³⁄₄in (146mm) diameter plastic-canvas circle
4¹⁄₄in (106mm) diameter plastic-canvas circle
   with one bar cut from the outer edge
Paterna Stranded Wool (Yarn)
   five skeins: 263 cream
18in (500mm) of 1in (23mm) wide pink ribbon
18in (500mm) of 1in (23mm) wide patterned
   ribbon

From the plastic canvas, cut one side 82 x 8 bars
and one inner crown 76 x 7 bars.

   Use three strands of wool (yarn) throughout,
and leave the eighth bar from the edge uncovered.

   Make up the hat in the same way as for the
medium hat, omitting the embroidered band.
Cut the ribbon to fit around the crown of the
hat, adding ¹⁄₂in (13mm) at each end for the
seam. Join each piece of ribbon into a circle and
slip over the crown. Offset the ribbon so that the
pink ribbon shows behind the patterned ribbon.

SMALL HAT

MATERIALS

6 x 2in (150 x 50mm) plastic canvas, 7 bars per
   inch (25mm)
7 x 1in (175 x 25mm) plastic canvas, 10 bars per
   inch (25mm)
Two 3in (75mm) diameter plastic-canvas circles
   (one with four bars cut from the outer edge)
Paterna Stranded Wool (Yarn)
   three skeins: 263 cream
Anchor Pearl Cotton
   small quantities of: 216 green; 76 dark pink;
   74 light pink

From the 7-bar plastic canvas, cut one side 41 x
7 bars and one inner crown 34 x 6 bars. From
the 10-bar plastic canvas, cut one band 64 x 8
bars.

   Use three strands of wool (yarn) throughout,
and leave the fifth bar from the edge uncovered.
Use pearl cotton singly for the cross stitch,
doubled for the overcasting.

   Make up the small hat in the same way as the
medium hat.

The Cradle

*This charming cradle would be perfect for a tiny doll or as a gift for a
new baby. If the cradle is being made for a special occasion, rather
than as a toy, the bedding could be embroidered in more detail. The
quilt could feature an initial or a nursery motif in cross stitch, and the
pillow could have a border of tiny flowers to make it extra pretty.*

   *Square-mesh circles are used for the cradle ends, as these may be cut
to the required shape. The ends are made double to ensure a neat
finish on both sides.*

MATERIALS

4in (100mm) square of plastic canvas, 7 bars per
   inch (25mm)
Four 3in (75mm) diameter square-mesh plastic-
   canvas circles
Paterna Stranded Wool (Yarn)
   three skeins: 263 cream

Anchor Pearl Cotton No 5
   one skein: 76 pink or 161 blue
Two 5 x 4in (125 x 100mm) pieces of 'Linda' or
   other soft counted-thread fabric, 27 threads
   per inch (25mm)
8 x 4in (200 x 100mm) of fine cotton fabric
12in (300mm) square of wadding

From the plastic canvas, cut two sides 22 x 9 bars and one base 22 x 15 bars. From the fine cotton, cut one mattress piece 4 x 3in (100 x 75mm) and one pillow piece 5 x 4in (125 x 100mm).

Use the pearl cotton doubled and two strands of wool (yarn).

SIDES AND BASE

For the sides, work a line of alternating long and short cross stitch along the top edge of the canvas in pink or blue pearl. Work three rows of long cross stitch in cream. Work one row in pink or blue. Fill in with a line of alternating long and short cross stitch in cream. Cover the base with lines of long cross stitch in cream.

FOOTBOARD

Very carefully cut away the sides of two circles to give straight edges as shown. Cut off the upper five bars to give a straight edge. The remaining section should be twelve bars deep.

For the outer section, work a line of alternating long and short cross stitch in pink or blue along the upper straight edge of one piece. Fill in with cream wool (yarn). For the inner section, on the other piece, leaving TWO bars uncovered at each side edge, work a line of alternating long and short cross stitch in pink or blue along the upper edge.

FIG 10 *Inner cradle ends, partly cut*

Complete the embroidery in cream, leaving the fourth bar up from the base uncovered. The cradle base will be joined along this bar.

HEADBOARD

For the outer section, work a line of three long cross stitches along the first straight bar at the top, followed by a line of four stitches then a single stitch at each side. Fill in the curved top with small cross and straight stitches, as necessary, to give a good cover. Complete the embroidery in cream.

For the inner section, embroider as above, leaving two bars uncovered at each straight edge as for the footboard, and the fourth bar from the lower edge uncovered as before.

TO MAKE UP THE CRADLE

Overcast the two sides to the base. Overcast a short edge of each side to the inner foot section, taking the stitches over the vertical bar next to the straight edge. Overcast the base to the uncovered horizontal bar. Repeat for the headboard. Place the outer end sections in position, with the wrong sides facing and edge stitch all round.

FIG 11 *Construction of cradle*

CRADLE BEDDING

Make up the mattress and pillow as instructed in Chapter 11, pages 118–19.

For the quilt, work a $2\frac{1}{2}$ x $1\frac{7}{8}$in (65 x 50mm) rectangle of four-sided edge stitch in the centre of the two pieces of fabric. Work two rows of stem stitch inside this in pink or blue pearl. Cut two pieces of wadding slightly smaller than the quilt fabric. Oversew the two fabric sections together, using the same thread as used for the embroidery, and sandwiching the wadding in between.

– 2 –
Pincushions and Needlecases

PINCUSHIONS and needlecases offer some of the most rewarding practical projects for the embroiderer. Because they are small and quickly made, they are ideal projects for learning a new technique. Although made in a few hours, they nevertheless give lasting pleasure, not only to the maker but to those using them. When my mother died at the age of ninety-one, I found in her workbox the needlecase my brother had made for her at school more than sixty years before.

I once bought a needlecase at a craft sale. It was apparently made by a child, and was not really very neat or beautiful. I felt it would be adequate until I had time to make a replacement. Now, though I have several of my own design, I will not part with the original and it is still in constant use – a reminder of the effort and concentration expended by its unknown maker.

Pincushions and needlecases

Cotton Canvas Pincushion and Needlecase

Embroidery on cotton canvas is one of the oldest forms of needlework which has been widely used throughout the ages. The fabric is almost completely covered on both sides, so any items made by this method will be extremely hard wearing and will stand up to constant piercing by pins and needles for a very long time.

When working on cotton canvas, half cross stitch is recommended for the main embroidery to avoid distortion. It is usual to start at the centre of the chart and work outwards. However, for ease in counting, you may prefer to work the border first. In this case, start with the double cross stitch, and make sure this is correctly placed before continuing. The materials are sufficient for the pincushion and needlecase.

| ⁄⁄⁄⁄ | dark green | ||||| | pink | ◣◢◣◢ | light green |
| ==== | green pearl | ❖❖❖ | light green double cross | ···· | cream |

Cotton canvas pincushion

MATERIALS

10 x 12in (250 x 300mm) cotton canvas,
  14 threads per inch (25mm)
7 x 10in (175 x 250mm) lining fabric
13 x 5in (330 x 130mm) Vilene
6 x 3½in (150 x 90mm) flannel or Aida
Wool oddments or Terylene wadding
Paterna Stranded Wool (Yarn)
  five skeins: 601 dark green

two skeins: 263 cream
one skein each: 604 light green; 904 pink
Anchor Stranded Cotton (floss)
  one skein: 891 yellow
Anchor Pearl Cotton No 5
  two skeins: 214 light green
Dark green sewing thread
Embroidery frame

From the cotton canvas, cut a 6in (150mm) square for the pincushion and one piece 8 x 5½in (200 x 140mm) for the needlecase. From the lining fabric, cut a 5¼in square and one piece 8 x 5½in (200 x 140mm).

Separate the wool (yarn) and use two strands. Use the pearl cotton singly, and all six strands of the stranded cotton (floss).

PINCUSHION

Mount the canvas onto the frame. Work the embroidery in half cross stitch following the chart, starting at the centre and working outwards. Add the French knots in yellow stranded cotton (floss), referring to the photograph for position.

Remove the canvas from the frame and press from the wrong side. Trim the surplus canvas at the edge to ½in (13mm). Trim the corners leaving at least three threads of canvas for turning. Work edge stitch for cotton canvas, all round.

BACKING THE PINCUSHION

Cut a square of Vilene a little smaller than the canvas to fit just inside the edge stitch. Place the lining right side down with the Vilene centrally over it. Fold the seam allowances over the Vilene and press. Trim the corners and tack (baste) in place. Place over the embroidery, wrong sides facing, and tack (baste).

Using the dark green sewing thread slipstitch the lining in place, leaving a small opening for stuffing at the centre of one side. The stitches should lie between the embroidery and the edge stitch, and should be closely spaced. They will scarcely show on the right side. Stuff the pincushion and complete the slipstitching.

NEEDLECASE

Work as for the pincushion, but before working the edge stitch around the perimeter, shape the spine as follows: fold the canvas along the uncovered threads on one side of the spine, so that the holes line up. Work edge stitch to cover. Repeat for the second side. Prepare and stitch the lining in place as for the pincushion, omitting the stuffing.

Finish the edges of the flannel 'page' by working a line of herringbone stitch all round the outer edge, about ½in (13mm) from the edge. Turn the fabric over and work a second line on the reverse, over the first one. This gives a neat decorative edge on both sides. Start and finish the stitching on the reverse side at the centre fold line, where it will show least. Fray out the fabric to the stitching.

Finger mark the central fold of the flannel 'page', place inside the cover and stitch in place along the centre of the spine. Needles may be stored in the page and the cover linings.

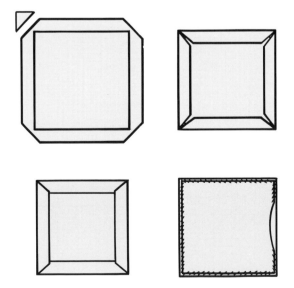

FIG 12 Making up a pincushion

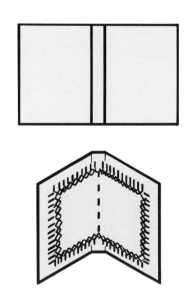

FIG 13 Making up a needlecase

light green wool

cream wool

pink wool

double cross stitch
light green wool

dark green wool

green pearl

pink wool

(left) Back and front (right) of needlecase

Pulled-work Pincushion and Needlecase

This traditional form of embroidery is usually worked in cream threads on cream fabric. The thickness of the thread used in the embroidery should be similar to the threads in the fabric. The stitches are worked at a tight tension, pulling the fabric into holes. The tighter the tension, the larger the holes become. The pulled-work areas may be combined with surface stitching, which is often very chunky, giving added beauty and texture to the work.

Many exquisite examples on very fine fabric have survived from the past. The examples given here are on a fairly coarse linen which has 18 threads to the inch (25mm). The stitches are very simple, so both the pincushion and the needlecase can be quickly made. The pincushion has decorative lines of stitching with spaces between. In the needlecase the bands of stitching are closer, giving a slightly different effect.

Various furnishing and dress fabrics are suitable for pulled work. The weave must be even in both directions, and easy enough to see. If choosing a light-coloured fabric, check that it is washable.

Three surface embroidery stitches are used here: stem, satin and raised chain band. Four-sided stitch is the only pulled-work stitch in the embroidery. A slightly different version of this is used for the edging. There are many other stitches which could be used to give a variety of interesting textures, once the pulled work is mastered.

Specialist books recommend working on a frame, as this makes counting easier and the tension more even. However, for the small pieces shown here, an embroidery frame is not absolutely necessary. The materials given are sufficient for both the pincushion and needlecase.

MATERIALS

13 x 12in (330 x 305mm) evenweave linen, 18 threads per inch (25mm)
10in (250mm) square of lightweight cotton or polyester cotton
9 x 8in (230 x 200mm) heavyweight Vilene
Terylene wadding or oddments of wool (yarn)
Anchor Pearl Cotton No 5
   three skeins: 926 cream
Anchor Stranded Cotton (floss)
   one skein: 926 cream
Embroidery frame (optional)

For the pincushion, cut two pieces 6in (150mm) square of evenweave linen, one piece 10 x 5in (250 x 125mm) of lightweight cotton, and one piece 8 x 5in (200 x 125mm) of Vilene. For the needlecase, cut one piece 9 x 7in (225 x 175mm) of evenweave linen, one piece 7⅝ x 4½in (190 x 115mm) of lightweight cotton and one piece 7 x 3⅞in (175 x 97mm) of Vilene.

Use pearl cotton singly and three strands of stranded cotton (floss).

Pulled-work pincushion and needlecase and circular pincushion box with pin compartment

PINCUSHION

Following the diagram and starting at the centre, work the pincushion embroidery. Remove from the frame, if using, and work four-sided edge stitch all round. The first line of thread to be pulled out should be four threads outside the embroidery.

To avoid mistakes in counting, pull out the threads and work the stitches on the first side only. Then sew each side in turn. Work four-sided edge stitch round the edge of the second piece, for the back, making it the same size as the first.

COMPLETING THE PINCUSHION

Place the two pieces together, right sides outside. Overcast to join around three sides, taking the stitches over the edge in each dip in the four-sided stitch.

Make a cushion pad a little larger than the embroidery (see Chapter 11, page 118). Slip the pad into the pincushion, and complete the slip-stitching to close the opening.

NEEDLECASE

The needlecase is made in two pieces, which are stitched together down one long edge on completion of the embroidery.

Embroider two pieces following the diagram. Work four-sided edge stitch all round both pieces. For this, the first thread to be removed should be four threads outside the embroidery.

Place the two sections together, wrong sides inside, and overcast down one long edge to join, taking the stitches through each dip in the edge stitch. Insert the lining and page as given in the canvas work needlecase.

FIG 14 Pulled-work pincushion

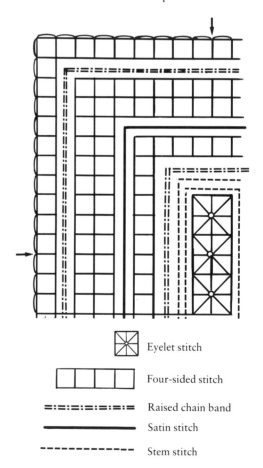

⊠ Eyelet stitch

▢▢▢▢ Four-sided stitch

=·=·=·=·=·=·= Raised chain band

⎯⎯⎯⎯ Satin stitch

- - - - - - Stem stitch

FIG 15 Pulled-work needlecase

Pulled-work Box Pincushion/Needleholder

This box pincushion is worked in natural fabrics but has a plastic-canvas lining instead of the usual card, to simplify the construction. The pulled-work top is attached to the canvas-work side, which is lined with plastic canvas to make a deep lid. The lid cleverly lifts off the base to reveal a pin box and needleholder. The needleholder fits inside the lid with a small pearl button for a handle.

In complete contrast to the traditional method of the previous pulled-work example, this pincushion top is embroidered ·with freehand pulled work, stitched on a loosely-woven lightweight fabric. No counting of threads is necessary, the stitches are just worked freely by eye combining the chosen colours to give a pleasing combination.

The example uses seven different colours of stranded cotton (floss), though fewer colours could be used if preferred.

MATERIALS

12 x 3in (300 x 75mm) cotton canvas, 12 threads per inch (25mm)

10 x 4in (250 x 100mm) plastic canvas, 7 bars per inch (25mm)

Three 3in (75mm) diameter plastic-canvas circles

6in (150mm) square of voile

8 x 4in (200 x 100mm) lightweight wool fabric

12 x 8in (300 x 200mm) cotton or polycotton lining fabric

Two pieces 8⅞ x 3in (220 x 75mm) lining fabric, cut on the bias

6 x 3in (150 x 75mm) heavyweight Vilene

7in (180mm) square of wadding

Anchor Stranded Cotton (floss)
   three skeins: 879 dark green
   one skein each of: 876 light green; 68 dark pink; 271 light pink; 118 dark iris; 95 light iris; 305 yellow

⅜in (10mm) diameter chunky pearl button

12 x 3in (300 x 75mm) of 1mm card

Clear adhesive

Vanishing pencil

Embroidery frame

4in (100mm) embroidery hoop

From the plastic canvas, cut one pincushion side 63 x 10 bars, one pincushion inner lid 56 x 4 bars and one pin box side 56 x 6 bars.

Use six strands of stranded cotton (floss) on the cotton canvas and twelve strands on the plastic canvas.

CANVAS SIDE STRIP

Mount the cotton canvas on to the frame. Leaving the first 1in (25mm) uncovered, work 9½in (238mm) in lines of long cross stitch as listed below. The first and last lines will need small infilling stitches along the edge. Follow the sequence:

1) dark green; 2) dark pink; 3) medium green; 4) light pink; 5) dark lilac; 6) dark green; 7) light lilac; 8) dark pink; 9) light green; 10) light pink; 11) dark lilac; 12) medium green; 13) light lilac; 14) dark pink; 15) dark green

Remove the canvas from the frame and press from the wrong side. Fold with right sides facing, and back stitch along the line of the embroidery to join into a ring. Check on the right side that the canvas does not show on the seam line. Press the seam, and turn to the right side. This sleeve will fit over the plastic canvas lining to form the lid side.

Work edge stitch in dark green along both edges, using the technique for cotton canvas (see Chapter 12, page 123).

FIG 16 Canvas work pincushion side

EMBROIDERED PINCUSHION LID

Mark the area to be embroidered on the lightweight fabric with a vanishing pencil. The area should be just a little larger than the plastic-canvas circle. Place the fabric in the hoop frame, ensuring that it is drum-tight. Work flower shapes in straight stitch, filling in with French knots to cover the marked area. Remove from the frame.

PREPARING THE LINING

Cut three circles of the cotton or polycotton lining fabric, and two of the wool fabric, to the size of the plastic-canvas circles plus 1/2in (13mm) extra all round for turnings.

Cut a circle of card slightly smaller than the plastic-canvas circles. The edge should be between the two outer bars, allowing room for the needle to pass through when embroidering the edge. Cover with lining fabric and slipstitch to a plastic-canvas circle. This is for the outer base of the box.

Trim one bar off the outer edge of a second plastic-canvas circle and cut two circles of card slightly smaller. Cover with lining fabric, one for the inside base of the pin box, the other for the underside of the pincushion section.

Cut two circles of Vilene to the same size as the covered card. Cover each with woollen fabric and slipstitch to each side of the trimmed plastic-canvas circle, for the needleholder.

Stitch the pearl button to the centre of one side. Needles may be stored on both sides.

PREPARING THE PINCUSHION

Cut a circle of lining fabric the size of the plastic-canvas circle plus 1/2in (13mm) turning all round. Cut a circle of card slightly smaller than the plastic-canvas circle. Cut four circles of wadding, one the size of the plastic-canvas circle, and the other three in decreasing size.

Run a line of small running stitches round the outer edge of one circle of lining fabric, 3/8in (10mm) in from the edge. Fasten on securely, but do not fasten off.

FIG 17 Padding the pincushion

Place the lining circle right side down and put the largest circle of wadding centrally over it. Add the other three wadding circles in order of decreasing size. Place the card circle over this. Draw up the stitching so that the card and wadding are enclosed. Check that there is sufficient wadding to give a good domed effect, adding more if necessary. This padded circle should be a loose fit inside the cotton canvas side, so that when it is covered with the embroidery it fits snugly. Try the circle in position, as the size of the card could be adjusted if necessary at this stage. If all is well, pull up the stitching really tightly and fasten off securely.

Using a plastic-canvas circle as a guide trim the pulled-work embroidery into a circle allowing at least 1in (25mm) extra all round. Sew a line of running stitches around the edge without fastening off, as before. Place this right side down with the prepared pad over it, also right side down. Pull up the stitching tightly as for the lining, and fasten off securely.

TO MAKE UP THE PINCUSHION

For the main lining, overlap the plastic canvas (63 x 10) for the pincushion side by four bars and stitch securely in place to form a ring. Try this inside the cotton canvas sleeve, to make sure the size is correct, and adjust the overlap if necessary.

Join one of the bias strips of lining fabric into a ring, press the seam, and place inside the plastic canvas, adjusting the length if necessary. Turn the edges to the outside, and tack (baste) in position. Slip this inside the cotton canvas sleeve. The lower edge of the plastic canvas should be level with the edge of the canvas, the upper edge slightly lower. Slipstitch all round the lower edge using three strands of dark green. Remove the tacking (basting).

PINCUSHION LID INNER SIDE

Overlap the short edges of the plastic canvas (56 x 4) by four bars and stitch securely together to form a ring. Overcast the top edge. Any yarn will do as this will not be visible, it is just to give a key to the adhesive. Place the ring against the wrong side of the smaller fabric-covered circle, and overcast to join, making a shallow box shape.

FIG 18 Lining the pincushion

FIG 19 Pincushion lid and assembly

Spread adhesive around the top edge of the box and around the edge of the base of the pincushion. Place the pincushion over the box section and allow to bond.

Spread adhesive inside the embroidered pincushion side and place the box inside with the edges level. Hold in place until bonded.

THE PIN BOX

Turn under about ¼in (5mm) on one long edge of the bias strip for covering the pin box side. Place the fold close to the lower edge of the plastic canvas (56 x 6) and slipstitch in place, trimming the short ends to ⅜in (10mm). Turn the ends over the plastic canvas. Place the two short edges together, wrong sides facing, and overcast securely to join into a ring. The join may poke slightly, but this method avoids bulk.

FIG 20 Pin box

Place the ring over a plastic-canvas circle and overcast to join to the bar next to the edge of the circle. Fold the free edge of the fabric to the inside and smooth the spare fabric over the base.

Edge stitch all round the outer bar of the base with twelve strands of green stranded cotton (floss) using the plastic canvas technique (see Chapter 12, pages 122-23).

Slip the smaller lined card circle inside the box. When closing the pin box place the needle holder on the pin box, button side down, then place the embroidered pincushion lid on top.

Fabric and Plastic Canvas Pincushion and Needlecase

For this matching pincushion and needleholder set, the flower motif has been covered with embroidery worked in matching stranded cotton (floss). The same fabric, without embroidery, is used for lining the needlecase – cut to display the flower motif in the centre of the cover. The sides of the pincushion and the frame of the needlecase are worked on plastic canvas, in colours to tone with the embroidery.

MATERIALS

10 x 6in (250 x 150mm) plastic canvas, 10 bars
    per inch (25mm)
15 x 4in (380 x 100mm) patterned fabric
15 x 4in (380 x 100mm) Vilene
12in (300mm) square of wadding
Anchor Stranded Cotton (floss)
    two skeins in each of your chosen colours

Colours are not given as they will depend on the fabric. The materials given are sufficient for both pincushion and needlecase.

From the plastic canvas, for the pincushion cut four sides 28 x 9 bars and two pieces for the top and base 28 bars square. For the needlecase, cut two sides 30 x 24 bars and one spine 30 x 3 bars.

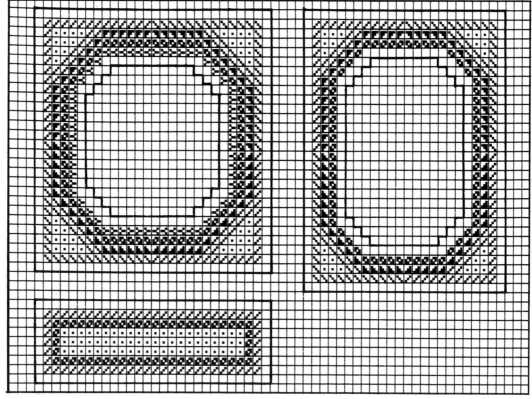

(left) pincushion and (right) needlecase

*Fabric and plastic-canvas pincushion and needlecase and
hat-shaped thimble holder and needlecase*

Use twelve strands of cotton (floss) for the tent stitch and six for the edge stitch on plastic canvas. Use three strands on the fabric.

Embroider the flowers on the fabric by outlining the shapes in stem stitch and then filling in with straight stitch, working French knots at the centre of the flowers.

Embroider the plastic canvas. Put in extra stitches on the slanting lines at each corner where the canvas will be cut. This avoids filling in these gaps when working the overcasting.

Very carefully cut out the inner uncovered areas, taking care to leave one bar all round beside the embroidery. Overcast the inner edges.

PREPARING THE FABRIC

Vilene: Cut one square just slightly smaller than the plastic canvas for the pincushion top. Cut two pieces the size of a single needlecase cover. Cut one piece the size of the inside of the needlecase, across the spine and both covers.
Fabric: Cut the embroidered panels a fraction smaller than the outer edge of the plastic canvas. Press on the wrong side.
Wadding: Cut three pieces for the pincushion, one the size of the Vilene, one slightly smaller and the third smaller still. Cut six pieces for the needlecase, two the size of the aperture, two slightly smaller and two smaller still.

TO MAKE UP

Place the fabric for the pincushion, right side down with the pieces of wadding on top in order of size, largest first, followed by the square of Vilene. Use running stitches to join the three layers together, just inside the edge. Position these stitches so that they will not show when the embroidered frame is placed over them, Test behind the frame to make sure there is sufficient wadding to dome the fabric nicely.

More may be inserted if wished. Glue or stitch in position on the back of the frame section. Prepare the needlecase covers in the same way.

Stitch the sides of the pincushion to the top and join the corners to form a box shape. Attach the prepared base, stuffing with wadding before completing the stitching.

Join the covers of the needlecase to the spine and edge stitch all round. Cut and insert the lining and page, as in the cotton canvas version on page 24.

Hat-shaped Thimble Holder and Needlecase

Imported hat-shaped needlecases were popular when I was a child. This modern version is stronger and more hard wearing than they were, and, as it takes very little time to make, it would be ideal as a small gift or bazaar item.

MATERIALS

4 x 3in (100 x 75mm) plastic canvas, 10 bars
    per inch (25mm)
Three 3in (75mm) diameter plastic-canvas circles
Anchor Stranded Cotton (floss)
    four skeins: 118 iris
    one skein: 926 cream
7 x 4in (180 x 100mm) lightweight cotton or
    polycotton lining fabric
7 x 4in (180 x 100mm) heavyweight Vilene

From the plastic canvas, cut one side piece 35 x 9 bars, one lining 31 x 9 bars and one hinge 14 x 3 bars.

Use twelve strands of cotton (floss) for the satin, tent and edge stitch, six elsewhere.

CROWN LINING

Leaving the first and last four bars of the plastic canvas uncovered, work alternating lines of tent and satin stitch in cream across the hat lining (31 x 9).

Overlap the uncovered ends, right side inside, matching the bars, and tack (baste). Complete the embroidery through both layers, joining into a ring. Edge stitch both edges.

SIDE

Leaving the first and last four bars of the plastic canvas uncovered, work a line of tent stitch down one long edge of the side canvas (35 x 9) in cream stranded cotton (floss). Next work a line of sloping satin stitch over three bars, and another line of tent stitch. Then work a line of long cross stitch in iris. Overlap and complete through both layers.

HINGE

Work a central line of tent stitch in iris, then overcast all round the outer edge.

CIRCLES

For the base, starting at the outer edge, cover one circle as follows:

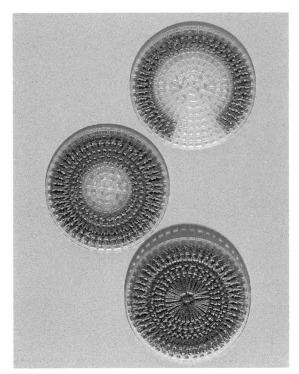

FIG 21 Base, brim and crown of hatbox

1) a line of tied cross stitch over three bars next to the edge
2) a round of straight stitch over one bar
3) a round of cross stitch
4) satin stitch into the centre, using six strands
5) a cross stitch over the centre intersection

Work rounds of back stitch between the lines of stitching where necessary, to fill in and give a good cover. Finally edge stitch all round.

For the brim, work rounds 1, 2 and 3 as above on another circle. Leaving one bar beside the embroidery, cut out the centre of the circle. Edge stitch around the outer edge of the brim.

For the crown, embroider a cross at the centre of the third circle, surrounded by satin stitch over two bars. Cut out, leaving one bar outside the embroidery. Keep the outer part of the circle intact, as it will be used as a guide for cutting the Vilene and lining. Back stitch between the outer bar and the embroidery.

TO MAKE UP

Overcast the hat crown to the hat side. Place the hat side in position over the brim, with uncovered edges matching, and overcast in place

using twelve strands of cream stranded cotton (floss).

Cut one bar from the outer edge of the frame circle left after cutting the hat crown. Cut two circles of Vilene the same size, but without the hole at the centre. Cut two circles of lining fabric, adding 5/8in (15mm) turning all round.

Place one piece of lining fabric right side down with a piece of Vilene centrally on top. Turn the edges over and tack (baste) using small stitches, smoothing the edge as you go to avoid bulges. Slipstitch the lining to the hat base using three strands of iris stranded cotton (floss). Remove the tacking (basting).

Using the plastic-canvas circle as a guide, mark the central hole with a hard pencil on the second piece of Vilene. Cut out the centre. Cover the Vilene with lining as above. Snip the exposed fabric at the centre and carefully snip at intervals to the edge of the Vilene.

Slipstitch the lining under the hat brim around the outer edge, pushing the spare fabric at the centre into the crown. Slip the embroidered lining into the hat, pushing the spare lining smoothly inside. There is no need to stitch.

Overcast the hinge to the hat base and brim using three strands of iris cotton (floss).

FIG 22 Assembly of hatbox

– 3 –
Victorian-style Boxes

*P*LASTIC canvas really comes into its own when making boxes, as no seam allowances are needed so construction is very easy. Ultra-stiff canvas may be used instead of card for the lining, to make the box completely washable.

The boxes in this chapter are based on Victorian designs, although the originals were usually covered in paper and often had photographs inset. The sides are hinged to the base so that they fall open when the lid is removed, giving easy access to the contents.

Although they may look complicated, they are actually very easy to make. The secret of success lies in making the card lining just the right size, so that when the box is closed the sides fit together neatly, without bulging.

Mini basket, square sewing box, pin box and dressing table box

Square Sewing Box

This box uses plastic canvas for the main structure and fabric-covered card for the lining, and has a matching pin box and mini basket. The design could easily be reduced or enlarged to suit other sizes, or stitched in light colours on a dark background for a different effect.

MATERIALS

10 x 9in (250 x 230mm) plastic canvas, 10 bars
  per inch (25mm)
36 x 3½in (900 x 90mm) lining fabric
17 x 3in (400 x 80mm) wadding
7in (180mm) square of 2mm card
8 x 7in (200 x 180mm) 1mm card
20in (500mm) of ¼in (5mm) wide ribbon
Clear adhesive or Copydex
Paterna Stranded Wool (Yarn)
  seven skeins: 263 cream
Anchor Pearl Cotton No 5
  three skeins each of: 216 green; 895 pink
  one skein: 305 yellow

From the plastic canvas, for the outer box cut
one base 27 x 27 bars, four sides 30 x 27 bars,
one lid 29 x 29 bars and four lid sides 29 x 7
bars. For the inner box, cut one base 12 x 12
bars and four sides 22 x 12 bars. For the thimble
box, cut five pieces 9 x 9 bars. From the 2mm
card, cut four sides 2¾ x 2⅜in (70 x 63mm).
From the 1mm card, cut four inner box sides
2 x ¹⁵/₁₆in (50 x 24mm), two base pieces 2½in
(64mm) square and one inner lid 2¾in (70mm)
square.

Use the pearl cotton singly for the cross
stitch, doubled for tent stitch. Use a single
strand of wool (yarn) for the small cross stitch
and two strands elsewhere. Embroider following the charts.

PREPARING THE LINING

Using the card pieces as a guide, cut out the lining fabric, allowing ⅝in (15mm) extra all
round for turnings. Cut out eight pieces of
wadding the same size as the 2mm card sides.

Place a piece of lining fabric right side down
on a flat surface with the wadding centrally over
it and the card on top. Trim the corners. Spread
adhesive evenly along the edges of the card.
Fold over the turnings and press into place all
round, pulling the fabric taut to avoid wrinkles
on the right side. Care should be taken to inset
the turnings at the corners to ensure that they
will not show later. Place a heavy book on top
and allow to bond. Line the other card pieces in
the same way.

Cut the ribbon to the width of each card side,
plus ½in (13mm) turnings. Place ribbon across

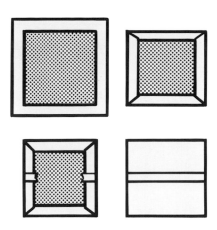

FIG 23 Lining of square sewing box

the centre of each side lining and glue the
surplus in place on the back.

TO MAKE UP THE SEWING BOX

Using the cream wool (yarn), edge stitch the
sides and upper edges of the eight embroidered

FIG 24 Stitching up the square sewing box

FIG 25 Gluing the square sewing box

green

pink

yellow

cream

cream/pink double cross
or cream double cross

Square sewing box

box sides. Place the lower edge of one large side section against the box base, wrong sides facing and edges matched up. Join with edge stitch to form a hinge. Repeat with the other three sides.

Attach the inner box sides to the inner box base in the same way, but with the wrong side of the sides against the right side of base.

Overcast the four sides of the thimble box to the thimble box base, with the wrong side of the sides against right side of base. Join the corners and overcast around the top edge.

Edge stitch the lid sides to the lid, and join the corners. Overcast all round the lower edge, matching the colours of the embroidery. Glue the prepared lining sections in position on the inside lid, and on both sides of the base. The edges should lie against the inside of the edge stitch. Glue the lining sections to the inside of the box sides.

Glue the thimble box to the inner box base. Glue the inner box to the box base placing it diagonally to the outer box base as shown.

Pin Box and Mini Basket

This little pin box and mini basket are designed to complement the Square Sewing Box in a matching set. The pin box is divided into two; one section is a padded pincushion, the other holds loose pins. The deep lid fits over both. The basket makes use of the circle of plastic canvas left over when the pin box lid is cut out.

MATERIALS

PIN BOX

9 x 4in (230 x 100mm) plastic canvas, 10 bars per inch (25mm)
Three 3in (75mm) diameter plastic-canvas circles
6 x 4in (150 x 100mm) cotton canvas, 14 threads per inch (25mm)
12 x 3½in (300 x 90mm) lining fabric
9 x 3in (230 x 75mm) wadding
6in (150mm) square of 1mm card

MINI BASKET

7 x 3in (175 x 75mm) plastic canvas, 10 bars per inch (25mm)
3in (75mm) diameter plastic-canvas circle with three bars cut from the outer edge

FOR BOTH ITEMS

Paterna Stranded Wool (Yarn)
    five skeins: 263 cream
Anchor Pearl Cotton No 5
    two skeins each of: 895 pink; 216 green
    a small amount of: 305 yellow
    sewing thread to match the lining

PIN BOX

From the plastic canvas, cut one box side 88 x 10 bars, one inner box side 79 x 9 bars, one backing strip 8 x 10 bars and another 8 x 9 bars, one divider 24 x 9 bars.

Use a single strand of wool (yarn) or pearl cotton for the cross stitch and edge stitch on the 10-bar mesh. Use the same wool (yarn) or cotton doubled for edge stitching around the circle and for the overcasting.

Tack (baste) the 8 x 10 backing strip to the right end of the plastic canvas side (88 x 10), under-lapping it by four bars (Fig 3). Leaving the first and last four bars uncovered, work the embroidery from the chart. Lap the left end over the backing strip and complete the embroidery through both layers, joining into a ring (Fig 4). Embroider the inner box side in the same way. Embroider the box divider, overcasting the short edges.

For the box top, using the pearl cotton doubled, work a line of cross stitch next to the outer bar of one circle. Alternate green and pink stitches. Cut out the centre of this circle to make a frame, leaving one bar beside the embroidery. Overcast the inner edge in cream.

Cut another plastic-canvas circle in half. Leaving three bars all round, cut out a semi-circular aperture from one of the sections for the pincushion. Work cross stitch in alternating green and pink. Overcast the inner edge in cream.

Embroider the cotton canvas following the chart on page 42, ensuring that the embroidery fills the frame for the top. Embroider an area of cotton canvas in cream tent stitch, to fill the semi-circular aperture.

PREPARING THE LINING

Cut three circles of card just a little smaller than the plastic-canvas circle, so that the edge comes halfway between the two outer bars. Cover two circles with fabric and set the third aside.

Cut three circles of wadding, one the size of the lid embroidery, one slightly smaller and another smaller still.

TO MAKE UP THE PIN BOX

Press the canvas from the wrong side. Trim all

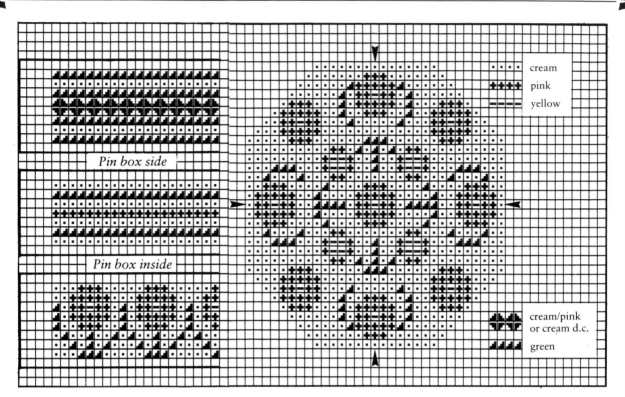

cream

pink

yellow

Pin box side

Pin box inside

cream/pink
or cream d.c.

green

Mini basket

Cotton canvas pinbox top

round so that the edge is just inside the outer edge of the prepared plastic-canvas frame. Glue sparingly around the wrong side of the frame and place it carefully over the embroidery. Ease the cotton canvas up slightly to allow for the doming effect when it is padded. The ring of flowers round the outer edge should be just visible. Hold the frame in position until bonded. Overcast the embroidered lid to the box side. Overcast around the lower edge.

Place the circles of wadding in order of size centrally on the wrong side of one fabric-covered card circle, smallest first. Glue all round the outer edge. Press into position inside the pin box lid, and hold until bonded. The wadding should make the cotton canvas dome slightly. Glue the pincushion cotton canvas in

FIG 26 Assembly of the pin box

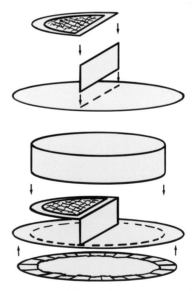

FIG 27 Assembly of the base of pin box

Mini basket and pin box

position in the half circle frame.

Place the divider across the centre of a circle of plastic canvas and stitch into position using cream wool (yarn). Overcast the inner box side to the base, taking the stitching over the bar next to the edge. Using toning sewing thread, stitch the second covered card circle to the underside of the base. Place the embroidered half circle in position over one half and overcast into place, stuffing with wadding before completing. Continue the stitching to overcast the other half section.

Cut the remaining card circle in half, and trim as necessary to fit the pin box. Cover with lining fabric and slip into place, to complete.

MINI BASKET

From the plastic canvas cut one side 68 x 10 bars, one lining 62 x 9 bars and one handle 54 x 4 bars.

Make the mini basket following the instructions in Chapter 1 for the Circular Basket, following the chart opposite.

Dressing Table Box

This box is made in a similar way to the sewing box but the lid sides lie flush with the sides of the box when closed. The central box is designed to hold spare buttons together with needles and thread for emergency repairs. The inside of the pin box lid is padded, so it can be used as a pincushion. The small compartments of this useful box would make it equally suitable for storing jewellery.

It is best to decide what you wish to keep in the box before cutting out the plastic canvas so that the compartments can be cut to size. The small side pockets at the centre of the long sides are designed to support the sides when the box is closed. If you wish to store large items, these could be omitted to give extra space.

MATERIALS

One 14 x 11in (355 x 280mm) sheet of plastic canvas, 10 bars per inch (25mm)
18 x 7in (450 x 180mm) lining fabric
8 x 6in (200 by 150mm) wadding
6 x 5in (150 x 125mm) 2mm card
11 x 6in (280 x 150mm) 1mm card
36in (900mm) of ⅛in (3mm) wide ribbon
Clear adhesive or Copydex
Paterna Stranded Wool (Yarn)
  four skeins: 494 flesh
Anchor Pearl Cotton No 5
  four skeins: 896 dark pink
  one skein each of: 894 medium pink; 893 light pink; 216 green; 305 yellow

From the plastic canvas, for the outer box, cut a base and lid 57 x 33 bars each, two sides 57 x 13 bars and two sides 33 x 13 bars, two lid sides 57 x 7 bars and two lid sides 33 x 7 bars. For the inner box, cut two sides 51 x 10 bars and two sides 21 x 10 bars, two dividers 20 x 10 bars and one 10 x 10 bars, two outer pockets 19 x 10 bars and four 3 x 10 bars. For the thimble boxes, cut ten pieces 9 x 9 bars. For the pin box lid, cut a lid and lid facing 21 x 21 bars each, one underlid 17 x 17 bars and four lid sides 17 x 4 bars.

Use pearl cotton singly and two strands of wool (yarn). For the card pieces, see Preparing the Lining on page 46.

OUTER BOX

For the sides, using the dark pink pearl start at the top left corner with a small cross stitch and then work 10 long cross stitches diagonally down to the right. Continue in zig-zag as shown

FIG 28 Zig-zag stitch

Dressing table box

in the photograph, finishing with a small cross stitch. On each side of this line work a line in light pink, then a line in flesh wool (yarn). Next fill in the triangles with dark pink. Work edge stitch round the sides and the top edge in dark pink.

For the lid sides, work a line in long cross stitch in dark pink, followed by one in light pink, one in flesh wool (yarn), and finish with a line in dark pink.

For the lid, work the corners in long cross stitch using the photograph as a guide. Embroider the floral centre in small cross stich, following the chart on page 46.

INNER BOX

For the box base, work a border in tent stitch with flesh wool (yarn).

For the inside box, embroider the long sides following the flower border chart. Work the

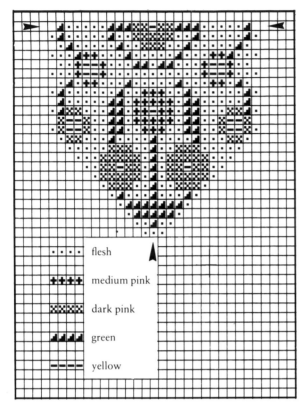

· · · ·	flesh
+++++	medium pink
✗✗✗✗✗	dark pink
◢◢◢◢◢	green
‒‒‒‒‒	yellow

Centre of dressing table box lid

two short sides and the outer pockets with two flower shapes. Start at the centre and work outwards, covering the extra bar at each end of the short sides with cross stitch. Work a line of tent stitch to cover the four outer pocket sides.

For the dividers and thimble boxes, cover each piece with tent stitch in light pearl cotton.

Cover the four pin box lid sides (17 x 4) with tent stitch in flesh wool (yarn). Embroider the pin box lid (21 x 21) following the chart opposite. Work a line of tent stitch in flesh wool (yarn) around the edge of the second square (21 x 21).

Work a line in dark pink pearl around the outer edge of the underlid square (17 x 17). Cut away the central uncovered area taking care to leave one bar beside the embroidery to form a frame. Edge stitch this inner edge in flesh wool (yarn).

PREPARING THE LINING

From the 2mm card, cut two pieces 5½ x 1½in (138 x 38mm) and two pieces 3 x 1½in (76 x 38mm). From the 1mm card, cut a lid and outer base 5½ x 3in (140 x 76mm) each, four pieces 1⅞ x ⅞in (48 x 22mm) and four pieces 1¹³/₁₆ x ⅞in (46 x 22mm), and two pieces 1¹³/₁₆in (46mm) square.

Line the four pieces of 2mm card for the outer sides as for the Square Sewing Box. Because the box lining extends above the embroidered side, the turning at the top needs to be sufficiently deep to give a neat finish. Add strips of ribbon across the centre of each piece.

Line the 1mm card for the lid and the outer base and the eight pieces of card for the inner compartments. Cut a piece of lining fabric 1⅝in (40mm) square for the pincushion.

TO MAKE UP THE BOX

Slipstitch a section of lined card to the lid. Edge stitch the lid pieces into a box shape, then edge stitch all round the lower edge with dark pink.

Overcast the outer pocket sides (10 x 3) to the inner box sides over the uncovered bars of plastic canvas. Overcast the sides to the base over the bar next to the tent stitch and join the corners. Overcast the outer pockets to the base and join the corners. Overcast the dividers in place.

Stitch the thimble sections into two box shapes of five squares each and place in position in the smaller compartment of the inner box. Edge stitch the top edges, joining the thimble boxes as you go. Slipstitch the lined card to the outer base.

Glue the prepared box linings in place, the longer ones first, and slip in the base linings.

Place one pin box underlid side against the lid facing, with one long edge against the bar next to the tent stitch. Overcast to join. Repeat with the other three sides. Join the four corners to make a shallow box shape. Place the pin box lid on top of the underlid, with wrong sides facing, and edge stitch in dark pink to join.

Spread adhesive evenly round the inside of the prepared underlid frame. Place pincushion lining fabric centrally on the frame and allow to bond, easing out fabric to avoid wrinkles. This could be stitched in place if preferred. Edge stitch the frame section to the lid, stuffing with wadding before completing the stitching.

Edge stitch the box sides to the base. To complete the box, glue the box side linings in place.

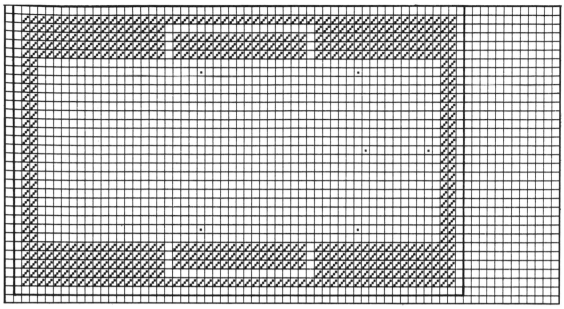

(above) Base of dressing table box   *(below) Dressing table box interior*

| | flesh | | medium pink | | green |
| | flesh | | dark pink | | yellow |

– 4 –

Embroidered Boxes

$\mathcal{Y}$OU can make many shapes or sizes of box using the ultra-stiff plastic canvas now available. It may be used for the outer box, or as a stiff lining to give rigidity as in the circular box shown here. However the ultra-stiff canvas is not suitable for making very small circular boxes, as it will snap when bent into a tight ring.

The patterns for boxes shown here could be easily adapted to different sizes. For instance, 7-bar plastic canvas could be substituted for 10-bar canvas, and larger circles could be used for the circular box, adapting the embroidery design as necessary.

Once you have mastered the art of box making it is relatively simple to adapt the method for making up in a natural fabric if this is preferred. The embroidered sections would need to be stretched around card before assembling.

Very small boxes do not need to be lined, but you should take extra care to keep the inside neat, and they should be assembled with the right side of the base inside the box. When lining a box with card you should choose the right thickness of the card for the box. While 1mm card is suitable for very small boxes, 2mm card gives a good rigid finish for larger ones.

Fitted circular box, travel sewing box, three nesting boxes and gold initial box

Fitted Circular Box

For a different effect, stitching with ribbon gives a lovely rich look to the embroidery. For maximum sheen the ribbon should lie flat on the surface.

    This box is a decorative way of keeping essential sewing items to hand. Keep one in your living room and you will never be without access to a needle and thread.

MATERIALS

6in (150mm) square of cotton canvas, 12 threads
   per inch (25mm)
14 x 4in (355 x 100mm) plastic canvas, 10 bars
   per inch (25mm)
13 x 6in (330 x 150mm) ultra-stiff plastic canvas,
   7 bars per inch (25mm)
Four 4¼in (110mm) diameter plastic-canvas
   circles
Lightweight cotton or polycotton lining fabric,
   bias cut
   one piece 13¼ x 3¼in (335 x 80mm)
   one piece 15 x 5in (380 x 125mm)
16 x 8in (400 x 200mm) of wadding
15 x 5in (380 x 125mm) 1mm card
Clear adhesive or Copydex
Anchor Pearl Cotton No 5
   five skeins: 400 charcoal
   one skein: 398 light grey
Anchor Stranded Cotton (floss)
   five skeins: 387 cream
   two skeins: 860 green
1.5mm wide Offray ribbon
   3¼yd (3m): 168 colonial rose
   4⅜yd (4m): 447 iris
   3¾yd (3.5m): 660 yellow
Sewing thread to tone with the lining fabric

From the 10-bar plastic canvas, cut one side
132 x 23 bars and one backing strip 8 x 23 bars.
From the 7-bar plastic canvas, cut one lining
piece 89 x 13 bars, one lid rim 85 x 3 bars, one
tray support 85 x 6 bars, one tray side 82 x 6
bars, one tray divider 25 x 6 bars and one 13 x 6
bars. From the wadding, cut one side piece 7 x
3½in (180 x 90mm), and put the remainder on
one side.

Use pearl cotton doubled for the embroidery
and singly for the edge stitch on the 10-bar
plastic canvas. Use twelve strands of the
stranded cotton (floss).

THE SIDE

For details on sewing with ribbon, see Chapter
11, page 117.

Tack (baste) the backing strip (8 x 23) to the
right end of the side piece of plastic canvas
(132 x 23), underlapping it by four bars. Leaving four bars uncovered at each end work the
embroidery from the example. Lap the left end

FIG 29 Ribbon box side pattern

over the right to form a ring and complete the
embroidery through both layers.

THE LID

Work a line of tent stitch in light grey pearl over
the bar next to the edge of one plastic-canvas
circle. Very carefully cut out the inner uncovered area, taking care to leave one bar inside
the stitching. Trim off the spikes and edge stitch
in charcoal pearl. Work a line of tent stitch in
charcoal over the bar next to the edge of a
second circle.

Leaving the first and last four bars uncovered, work a line of tent stitch in charcoal
along the lid rim (85 x 3) bars. Overlap the ends
and complete the stitching through both layers.

Work the embroidery on the cotton canvas,
filling in the cream background as necessary to
fill the aperture when the frame is placed over it.

THE FITTINGS

For the tray support, leaving the first and last
four bars uncovered, embroider the strip of
plastic canvas (85 x 6) with four lines of tent
stitch in charcoal pearl. Overlap the four bars at
each end and complete the embroidery through
both layers to join into a ring. Edge stitch both
edges.

For the tray side and dividers, embroider the
tray side in the same way as the support, working a line of tent stitch in light grey pearl along
the upper edge. Embroider the dividers, overcasting the short ends as you go.

FIG 30 Embroidery on cotton canvas

THE LINING

Overlap the plastic canvas for the lining (89 x 13) by four bars, matching up the holes, and tack (baste) securely in place. Tack (baste) the strip of wadding to the inside, trimming it to give a butt join and avoid bulk. Trim the edges of the wadding level with the plastic canvas.

FIG 31 Overlapping the side

Join the lining fabric into a ring taking a ½in (13mm) seam. Place this INSIDE the plastic canvas, wrong side against the wadding. Fold the upper turning to the outside and tack (baste) in place. The joining seam may be adjusted at

this point, if necessary. Turn the lower turning to the outside and tack (baste). Work herringbone stitch between the turnings to hold them in place. Remove the tacking (basting).

Cut two card circles slightly smaller than the plastic-canvas circles. The edge should be between the outer bar and the one next to it, to allow the needle to pass through when stitching. Cover one card circle with lining fabric and one with wadding and lining fabric.

FIG 32 Box lining

Cut two bars off the outer edge of one circle of plastic canvas. Cut three circles of card slightly smaller than this, as before. Cover one circle with lining and one with lining and wadding. The third circle will be used to line the tray.

THE UNDERLID

Overcast the rim to the plastic-canvas circle with the charcoal edge, taking the stitches over the bar next to the tent stitch. As there are more holes on the circle than on the rim you will need to work two stitches into one hole at intervals. Overcast the free edge.

Slipstitch the smaller covered card circle with the wadding inside the underlid, using the toning sewing thread.

FIG 33 Underlid preparation

THE UPPER LID

Place the frame with the light grey pearl tent stitch over the prepared embroidery and trim the canvas so that the edge is just inside the outer edge of the plastic canvas. Glue sparingly around the underside of the frame and place the embroidery in position behind it. Ease the canvas up slightly to allow for the doming effect when it is padded. The four flowers should be just visible. Hold in position until bonded.

Cut a circle of wadding the size of the lid em-

broidery, another one slightly smaller and another one smaller still. Place the underlid on the table, wrong side up. Place the smaller piece of wadding centrally over it, followed by the other two in order of size. Place the embroidered lid over the top and edge stitch all round in charcoal to join them. The wadding should make the canvas dome slightly.

TO MAKE UP THE BOX

For the box, slipstitch the larger covered circle of card without the wadding to a plastic-canvas circle. Place this lining side down, with the box side over it and edge stitch all round to join them, using charcoal pearl. Edge stitch round the top of the box side in charcoal.

Spread adhesive inside the box, close to the upper edge. Slip the prepared lining into position. Place clothes pegs or paper clips all round the edge to hold firmly until bonded. Slip in the second lined circle, followed by the tray support.

For the tray, place the longer divider on the trimmed plastic-canvas circle with the edge against the straight bar across the centre, to divide it in half. The line of light grey pearl should be along the upper edge. Overcast the divider in place along the base. Repeat with the shorter piece, dividing one half into quarters.

FIG 35 Tray

Slipstitch the smaller lined circle without the wadding to the underside of the tray. Place the prepared side over this and overcast the edges together with charcoal to form the tray. Edge stitch all round, catching in the top of the dividers as you go, then edge stitch the dividers in charcoal.

Cut the remaining card circle to fit these divisions, cover with lining fabric and place in the tray. Slip the tray into the box and it is ready to be fitted with your sewing things.

FIG 34 Lid preparation

Gold Initial Box

The embroidery for this box is worked in stranded cotton (floss) and a gold ribbon-type thread, in a mixture of smooth satin stitch and chunky Rhodes stitch. To give the design extra sparkle the initial is also outlined with beads. The variation in light and shade is obtained by working the satin stitch blocks in alternate directions.

MATERIALS

10 x 9in (250 x 225mm) plastic canvas, 10 bars per inch (25mm)
Two pieces 4³⁄₈ x 4in (112 x 102mm) 1mm card
13 x 5in (330 x 125mm) 2mm card
36 x 6in (900 x 150mm) soft cotton or polycotton lining fabric
1 oz (30g) gold cut beads
Fine needle for beading
Clear adhesive or Copydex
Anchor Stranded Cotton (floss)
   seven skeins: 386 cream
Three reels of gold Diadem metallic thread

From the plastic canvas, cut a lid and base 46 x 42 bars each, two sides 46 x 18 and two 42 x 18 bars. From the 1mm card cut an outer base and lid lining 4³⁄₈ x 4in (111 x 100mm). From the 2mm card cut one lid lining 4¹⁄₈ x 3³⁄₄in (105 x 95mm), one inner base 4¹⁄₄ x 3⁷⁄₈in (108 x 98mm), two sides 4³⁄₈ x 1⁵⁄₈in (111 x 42mm) and two sides 3⁷⁄₈ x 1⁵⁄₈in (98 x 40mm).

Use nine strands of stranded cotton (floss) for the satin stitch squares and six strands for edge stitching. Use the gold thread singly.

First work the border of Rhodes stitch around the lid (46 x 42). Work an extra stitch inside each corner.

Select your chosen initial and embroider this in Rhodes stitch in the centre. Fill in with satin stitch blocks worked in alternate directions, using the stranded cotton (floss).

Work straight stitch in gold between the satin stitch squares and around the initial, omitting the edges of the lid.

STITCHING WITH BEADS

To bead the embroidered initial, choose a fine needle that will pass through the hole in the beads. You can buy a special beading needle, which is long and fine.

Place some of the beads in a shallow dish. Thread the needle with the sewing thread and fasten securely behind the top left corner of the initial. Bring the needle through to the right side. Pick up several beads on the point of the needle and slide them down to touch the embroidery. Continue until you have about 1in (25mm) of beads on the thread. Take the needle through to the back and work several back stitches. Next move back to the left taking a stitch between every few beads to couch the thread down at intervals. Continue to outline the initial and then work lines of beading between the Rhodes stitches.

FIG 36 Beading

TO MAKE UP THE BOX

See Chapter 11 for more details on making a box with an attached lid.

Cover the thinner card with lining and the remaining card with lining and wadding. Slip-stitch one thin piece of card to the base (46 x 42). This will be the outer base.

Omitting the edge above the letter, edge stitch round three sides of the lid. Glue the second thin piece of card to the wrong side of the lid. Glue the padded lining to the centre.

Edge stitch the box sides to the base and join the corners. Edge stitch round three sides of the top edge, two short and one long. Edge stitch the lid to the box section.

Gold initial box and travel sewing box

Glue the two longer side lining sections into the box at the back and front. Repeat for the short sides. These fit between the longer lining sections. Slip the base lining inside, and your box is complete.

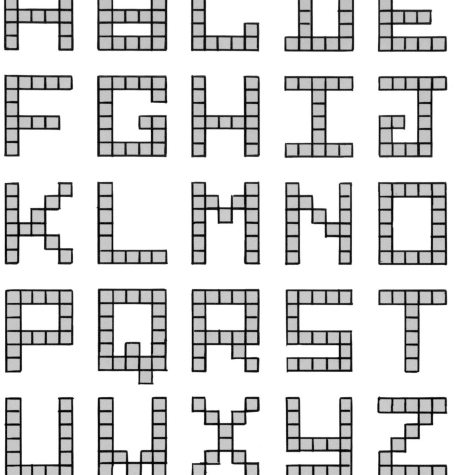

FIG 37 Beaded box letter chart

MAKING A TASSEL

Decide which thread or mixture of threads you wish to use and wind a quantity round three fingers. Slip the loops off. This will now be referred to as the tassel.

Take a length of thread, about 18in (450mm) long, double it and slip the folded end through the tassel, taking the ends through the loop and pulling tight. Thread both ends into the tapestry needle and stitch to the centre of the opening side of the box lid.

Wrap the thread around the tassel, about ¼in (6mm) down, and make a knot or two to secure the head. Take the ends down through the centre of the tassel and let them join the loop. Cut the loop and trim it to a suitable length.

FIG 38 Tassel

Travel Sewing Box

As this is a small, shallow box it can be lined with thin card, which also keeps it lightweight.

MATERIALS

9 x 6in (225 x 150mm) plastic canvas, 10 bars per
   inch (25mm)

9 x 6in (225 x 150mm) 1mm card

16 x 6in (400 x 150mm) lining fabric

$\frac{3}{8}$in (10mm) diameter button

Anchor Pearl Cotton No 5
   two skeins: 77 pink

1.5mm wide Offray ribbon
   10yd (9m): 815 cream
   17yd (15.5m): 275 wine

From the plastic canvas, cut a lid and base 42 x 42 bars each, and four sides 42 x 6 bars. From the 1mm card, cut two lid pieces $3^{15}/_{16}$in (99mm) square, two sides 4 x $\frac{3}{8}$in (100 x 10mm) and two sides $3^{15}/_{16}$ x $\frac{3}{8}$in (99 x 10mm).

Use the pearl cotton doubled for the embroidery, singly for the edge stitch.

Work the embroidery following Fig 39, referring to Chapter 11 for working with ribbon. For maximum effect the ribbon should lie flat on the surface. Stitch the button to the centre of one side. Make up as for the Gold Initial Box, omitting the second piece of lined card on the lid. Make a buttonhole loop with a tassel at the centre front of the lid.

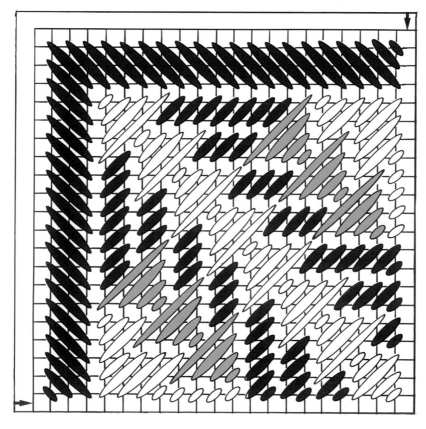

FIG 39 Stitch diagram travel sewing box

Three Nesting Boxes

These boxes are worked in a mixture of ribbon and stranded cotton (floss). Each box fits snugly into the next. They are not lined, so it is important to keep the embroidery on the inside as neat as possible. The materials given are sufficient for all three boxes. The chart for the flower pattern is on page 51, Fig 29.

MATERIALS

One 14 x 11in (355 x 280mm) sheet of plastic
   canvas, 10 bars per inch (25mm)
1.5mm wide Offray ribbon
   9yd (8m): 168 colonial rose
   20yd (18m): 447 iris
   2¼yd (2m): 660 yellow gold
Anchor Stranded Cotton (floss)
   nine skeins: 387 cream
   two skeins each of: 305 yellow; 118 iris;
   860 green
   one skein: 77 pink

From the plastic canvas, for the small box cut one lid 17 x 17 bars, four lid sides 17 x 6 bars, one base 15 x 15 bars and four base sides 15 x 5 bars. For the medium box, cut one lid 21 x 21 bars , four lid sides 21 x 8 bars, one base 19 x 19 bars and four base sides 19 x 7 bars. For the large box, cut one lid 25 x 25 bars, four lid sides 25 x 10 bars, one base 23 x 23 bars and four base sides 23 x 9 bars.

Use twelve strands of cotton (floss) for the embroidery and six for the edge stitch.

LARGE BOX

Work a single line of tent stitch in cream next to the outer edge of the square lid piece. Next work satin stitch in iris ribbon over two bars. As you work each stitch, hold the ribbon between finger and thumb and guide it through the canvas to keep it flat. (See Chapter 11 for further details of sewing with ribbon.) Fill in with the centre pattern from the example shown in Fig 29.

Work a line of tent stitch in cream around the outer edge of each side piece. Next work a line of satin stitch over two bars in iris ribbon. Fill in with satin stitch in yellow stranded cotton (floss).

Work the base in the same way as the lid, omitting the cream tent stitch around the edges.

FIG 40 Sides of the three nesting boxes

MEDIUM BOX

Work a single line of tent stitch in pink ribbon around the outer edge of the lid. Fill in the centre pattern following Fig 29.

Work a line of tent stitch in pink ribbon next to the edge of the four sides. Next work a line in cream. Fill in with iris stranded cotton (floss).

Work the base in the same way, omitting the pink tent stitch around the outer edges.

SMALL BOX

Embroider the lid following Fig 29, omitting the square of cream tent stitch around the edge. Work tent stitch in cream around the edge of the side. Fill in with satin stitch in pink ribbon.

Work the base as for the lid, omitting one line of the pattern at the edges.

TO MAKE UP THE BOXES

See Chapter 11 for details of how to stitch the boxes and lids together.

– 5 –
Country Cottage Desk Accessories

*T*HIS detailed model of a country cottage is in fact a desk tidy complete with pen holder and small shelves. The large sloping roof lifts to reveal the interior.

I first saw a picture of 'Corner Thatch' in a book of English cottages, looking for all the world like a tiny doll's house. It was built as a barn in the late-seventeenth century, and was later converted to a cottage. The contrast in colour and texture between the walls and the thatched roof, with the tiny splash of colour in the post box, just asked to be reproduced in some form of embroidery.

The stitched address book cover and stamp holder are worked in the same black, white and red to team with the cottage design.

A model could be made of any house or cottage, though most buildings will need simplifying. It is important to decide what are the salient features of the building, and then work out the size from these. I wanted my model of the cottage to be approximately to scale, and small enough to fit in my living room as a decorative feature. The main difficulty was keeping the size down, while retaining the essential details.

Desk accessories

The Cottage

The windows are the main feature of the front, so I started with these,
working a sample to decide how many bars of 10-bar plastic canvas
were needed to get sufficient detail. The timber sections were then
worked out in proportion to the windows. The same method was used
for the side walls. The resulting model is 10½ x 10 x 8in high (265 x
250 x 200mm). The hip ends of the roof were omitted to allow easy
opening of the box lid.

MATERIALS

Five 14 x 11in (355 x 280mm) sheets of plastic
  canvas, 10 bars per inch (25mm)
23 x 20in (585 x 510mm) 2mm card for lining
10½ x 7¾in (266 x 197mm) 1mm card for inner
  lining
18 x 12in (460 x 300mm) lightweight cotton
  lining fabric
60 x 12in (1.5m x 300mm) lightweight stretch
  velvet for lining
9⅝ x ⅜ x ⅛in (240 x 10 x 3mm) wood
Curved sewing needle
Clear adhesive or Copydex
Paterna Stranded Wool (Yarn)
  twenty skeins: 220 black
  ten skeins: 263 cream
  eight skeins: 200 dark grey
  seven skeins: 471 brown
  one skein: 950 red
Anchor Stranded Cotton (floss)
  two skeins each: 400 charcoal; 926 cream
  one skein each: 896 pink; 388 beige

THE FITTINGS

Two 18 x 12in (460 x 310mm) sheets ultra-stiff
  plastic canvas, 7 bars per inch (25mm)
17 x 10in (400 x 250mm) 2mm card

From the 10-bar plastic canvas, for the walls
and floor cut one front wall 97 x 43 bars, one
back wall 97 x 20 bars, two side walls 79 x 76
bars and one floor 97 x 79 bars.

For the bay window, cut one piece 23 x 14
bars, two pieces 17 x 5 bars, two bay supports
12 x 3 bars.

For the eaves, cut four pieces 78 x 3 bars, two
pieces 78 x 5 bars, four pieces 98 x 3 bars, two
pieces 98 x 5 bars, four pieces 46 x 3 bars and
two pieces 46 x 5 bars.

For the post box, cut one piece 32 x 12 bars,
two pieces 12 x 8 bars, two pieces 12 x 3 bars,
two pieces 27 x 6 bars and one piece 12 x 6 bars.

For the main roof, cut one piece 107 x 80 bars
and one piece 107 x 56 bars. For the roof edges
cut two pieces 107 x 3 bars, two pieces 80 x 3
bars and two pieces 56 x 3 bars. Cut two roof
coping pieces 107 x 8 bars, one roof ridge
107 x 6 bars and two gable ends 30 x 15 bars.

From the ultra-stiff mesh, for the shelves cut
two 62 x 32 bars, two 62 x 14 bars, and two
sides 31 x 33 bars. For the pen holder cut one
base 89 x 20 bars, one front 89 x 7 bars and two
sides 17 x 7 bars.

Use two strands of wool (yarn) unless otherwise stated. Use twelve strands of stranded
cotton (floss).

WALLS AND WINDOWS

Work the four walls in tent stitch unless
specified otherwise, following the charts on
pages 66-8. Trim the gable ends of the side walls
close to the embroidery, leaving complete bars
beside the stitches. Stitch the bay window pieces
following the charts on page 69. Also stitch the
sections for the post box.

ROOF

Cover each main section with brick stitch over
four bars, using one strand each of black,
brown and grey wool (yarn) in the needle.
Work satin stitch to cover the six narrow edge

FIG 41 Roof, stitching over the edge

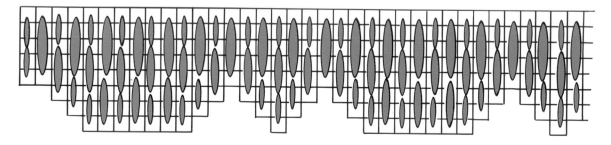

FIG 42 Coping

sections, taking the stitches over one edge (Fig 41), leaving the other edge uncovered for joining later. Embroider the ridge coping sections as shown in Fig 42. Cut away the uncovered canvas taking care to leave one bar beside the embroidery. Overcast the two short and the shaped edges in grey wool (yarn). Embroider the two gable ends and overcast all round with grey wool (yarn). Embroider the eaves in black wool (yarn), using satin stitch on the wide sections, tent stitch on the narrow.

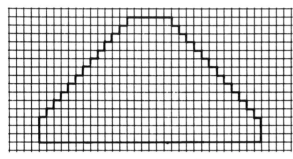

FIG 43 Gable ends

TO MAKE UP THE COTTAGE

Use two strands of dark grey wool (yarn) for stitching the roof together, elsewhere match the colour of the pieces being joined.

For the bay window, cut between the side windows and the central double window of the bay window section, trim off the spikes and overcast together again in cream. Trim the bay roof and base, leaving one complete bar of plastic canvas beside the stitching, and overcast to the window. Stitch the supports to each lower corner. Place in position on the door side of the house and stitch in place with black wool (yarn) along the base and top, cream wool (yarn) along the sides. Catch the supports in place at their lower end.

FIG 44 Construction of bay

For the post box, join the front to the sides and stitch the base in place. Join the roof sections together along one short edge. Overcast the narrow fascia pieces to the long edges of the roof, overcasting the two short edges of the roof as you do so. Catch stitch the roof section to the box, keeping the back edges in line with the side walls. Overcast the post box in position on the front wall of the house.

FIG 45 Post box

FIG 46 Eaves

FIG 47 Walls to base

For the cottage, stitch the eaves together in sets of three, one wide and two narrow pieces, along the long edges to form triangular sections, overcasting the short ends as you do so.

Overcast the four walls to the base. Join the four corners. Overcast all round the upper edge. Use three strands if this will pass through the canvas.

Using a single strand of black wool (yarn), stitch the eaves in position along the top of each wall, with edges matched up, and wide sloping faces uppermost.

For the roof, overcast the narrow edge strips to the roof along the side and lower edges.

Overcast the shaped edges of the two roof coping sections (107 x 8), using two strands of the dark grey wool (yarn), and tack (baste) to the edge of each roof section.

Overcast the roof edge with the shaped coping sections to the roof ridge (107 x 6), treating the two layers of the roof as one piece.

Catch stitch the shaped edges of the roof coping to the roof. Stitch the gable ends to the front roof and ridge end, using a single strand of dark grey wool (yarn).

FIG 48 Roof fascia   FIG 49 Coping sections

FIG 50 Roof

LINING THE COTTAGE

This process is very similar to that used in box making, and is not nearly so difficult as it might seem. Start when you are fresh, rather than at the end of a long hard day. Clear the table or worktop, reserving one section for a cutting board, one for gluing only, and one for leaving the glued sections while they are bonding.

Synthetic stretch velvet fabric, as recommended, is easy to handle and stretch over the card, does not crush or have a nap, and is not too bulky. Some synthetics do not take glue well, so leave them to bond before proceeding to the next step.

From the 1mm card, cut one piece 10½ x 7¾in (265 x 197mm).

From the 2mm card, cut one back wall 9½ x 2in (241 x 50mm), one front wall 9½ x 4¼in (241 x 108mm), two side walls 7⅞ x 7in (200 x 178mm), one floor 9½ x 7½in (241 x 190mm), one front roof 9¹¹/₁₆ x 4⅝in (246 x 117mm) and one back roof 9½ x 7in (241 x 178mm).

Try the pieces in position. The side walls go in first, the front and back fitting between them.

Mark the shaping needed on the side walls with a pencil. The top edges should be level with the embroidery on the back wall and the long sloping edges. They should be ³/₁₆in (4mm) lower than the ridge and short sloping side walls and the front wall. This allows the front roof lining to rest on the wall lining and be level with the embroidery. The lining should fit snugly without pushing the walls out. Any necessary adjustments should be made as you go along. Trim the side wall card to the required size and try in the cottage again.

Cover the 1mm card for the back roof with the cotton lining fabric and glue in position. Cover the remaining card with velvet, gluing sparingly, taking care to trim the corners to avoid bulk. Test the wall linings in the house once more, and if correct glue the turnings securely and glue the pieces into position. If wished, a layer of felt or wadding may be placed between the walls and the lining to give a more rounded appearance. Slip the covered floor section in place.

Stitch the front roof lining in place, right side to the interior. This should rest on the walls, giving a level surface for the embroidered roof to rest on. Glue the rear roof velvet lining in place. The edge should be ½in (12mm) away from the three outer edges of the fine lining and ¼in (6mm) from the hinge side.

Cover the strip of wood in cotton lining fabric, gluing the edges in place. Position across the ridge and glue at each end. Spread glue evenly on the front roof lining, place the roof in position and hold until bonded.

THE FITTINGS

Following the chart, cover the shelf supports with tent stitch, leaving the bars uncovered as shown. Overcast the long edges of the shelves

FIG 51 Front roof lining

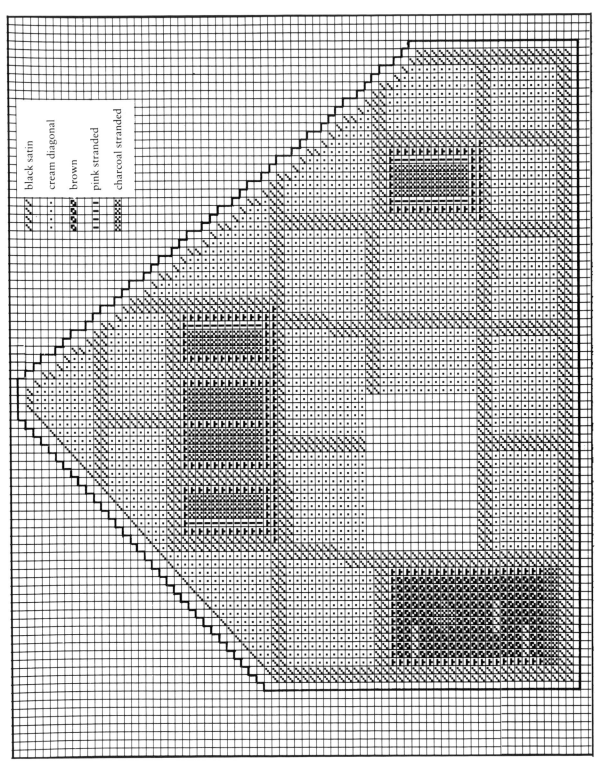

black satin
cream diagonal
brown
pink stranded
charcoal stranded

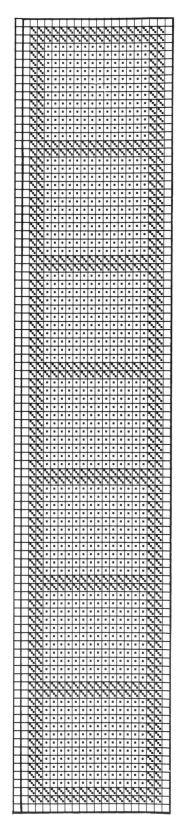

black satin

cream diagonal

beige stranded

cream stranded

charcoal stranded

(above) Back wall, (below) Front wall

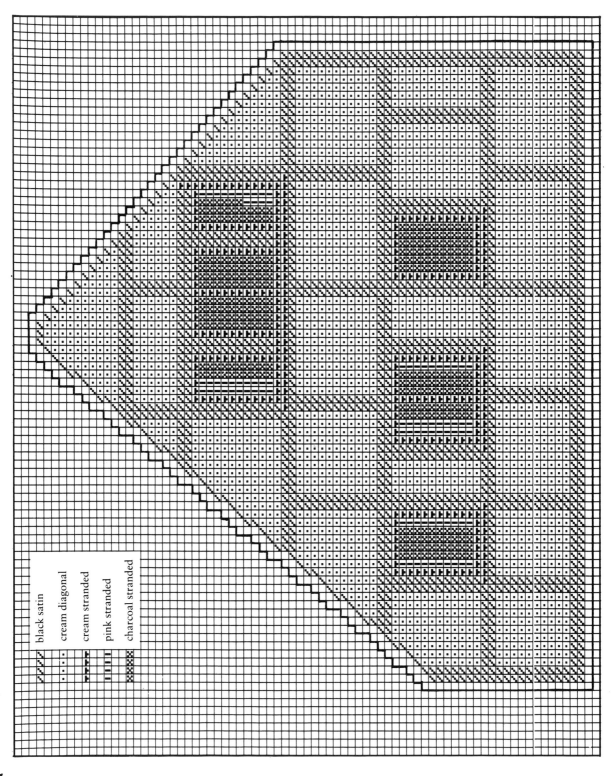

black satin

cream diagonal

cream stranded

pink stranded

charcoal stranded

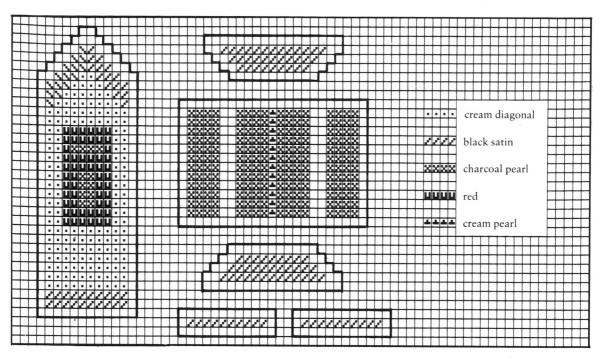

· · · ·	cream diagonal
////	black satin
✕✕✕✕	charcoal pearl
⊔⊔⊔⊔	red
▲▲▲▲	cream pearl

Post Box and bay window

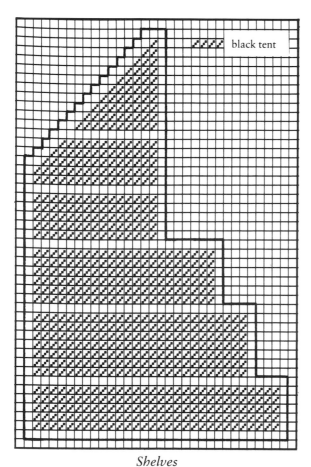

////	black tent

Shelves

and attach to the shelf supports at each end. Overcast remaining uncovered edges. Cut 2mm card to fit each shelf, cover with velvet and glue.

For the pen holder, work a single line of tent stitch in black around the outer edge of the base piece (89 x 20). Next work a line in red and then another in cream. Fill in the centre with lines of satin stitch over two bars in black. Across the plastic canvas for the front (89 x 7) work a line in cream, one in red, one in cream and two in black. Cover the two sides (17 x 7) with tent stitch. Overcast the back and the two sides to the base and join the front corners. Overcast all round the edges.

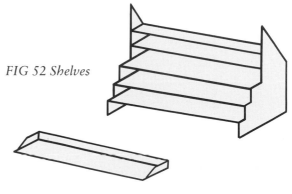

FIG 52 Shelves

FIG 53 Tray or pen holder

Address Book and Stamp Holder

To adapt the address book design to fit your own book, simply cut the plastic canvas to fit the covers, making them one bar wider all round than the cover. Cut a spine this length and 5 bars wide. Adapt the embroidery design as required.

MATERIALS FOR BOTH

11 x 14in (280 x 360mm) plastic canvas, 10 bars
   per inch (25mm)
Paterna Stranded Wool (Yarn)
   four skeins: 263 cream
   three skeins: 220 black
Anchor Pearl Cotton No 5
   three skeins: 46 red
   one skein each of: 209 green;
942 yellow

From the plastic canvas, for the address book cut two covers 64 x 36 bars, two stays 64 x 5 bars and one spine 64 x 3 bars. For the stamp holder cut two covers 36 x 29 bars, two pockets 34 x 15 bars and one spine 36 x 3 bars.

Use the pearl cotton singly for the cross and edge stitch. Use two strands of wool (yarn) for the tent stitch.

Embroider the covers in cross stitch following the chart and cover the stays and spine with cream wool (yarn) tent stitch. Overcast the long edges of the stays. Tack (baste) the stays in position inside the covers, about eight bars in from the outer edge.

Using the red pearl cotton, edge stitch the covers to the spine, then edge stitch all round the outer edge, attaching the stays as you work.

STAMP HOLDER

In order to avoid bulk the inside pockets of the holder are two bars narrower than the covers. Omitting the outer line of cross stitch along the top and base, embroider the covers and pockets from the chart and work a line of cross stitch in black down the spine. Overcast one long edge on each pocket section. Overcast to join the covers to the spine. Tack (baste) the pockets to the inside of the covers, long edges matched up. Work the outer line of black cross stitch, attaching the pockets as you do so. Overcast all round the outer edge.

(above) Address book, (below) Stamp holder

red
cream
black
green
yellow

– 6 –
Dolls' House Dining Room Furniture

*U*NTIL I visited a doll's house shop recently I had no idea of the fascination of this small world. There, in unbelievable detail, was everything one could possibly need in a real house, from chairs, tables and sofas down to candlesticks, books and antiques, all beautifully co-ordinated and arranged.

A varied range of furniture and kits is available from specialist suppliers, but by making your own you can introduce individual ideas, ensuring the uniqueness of your own dolls' house. Items from your own home could be copied if wished.

All the examples in the next three chapters are made to 1/12 scale. One foot (300mm) represents one inch (25mm). For example, a bed which usually measures 6ft 3in (1.90m) would measure 6¼in (160mm) in 1/12 scale.

The main embroidery uses 12 strands of stranded cotton (floss) throughout. This is rather expensive, and is not as easy to use as stranded wool (yarn), but gives a soft, smooth sheen closer to the texture of wood. To prepare the stranded cotton (floss), take a length of cotton about one yard or métre. Thread the needle, then knot the ends together.

Table, dining chairs, carver chairs and embroidered carpet

Dining Room Furniture

The table top, the back of the chairs, and the arms of the carvers have a double thickness of plastic canvas for extra stability. The materials given are sufficient for one table, two carvers, four dining chairs and the carpet.

MATERIALS

Four 14 x 11in (355 x 280mm) sheets of plastic canvas, 10 bars per inch (25mm)
9 x 6in (225 x 150mm) cotton canvas, 18 threads per inch (25mm)
8 x 6in (200 x 150mm) 1mm card
12 x 6in (300 x 150mm) wadding
Anchor Stranded Cotton (floss)
    44 skeins: 360 brown
    one skein each of: 387 beige; 860 green;
    896 pink; 847 cream
Anchor Pearl Cotton No 5
    three skeins: 216 green
    one skein each of: 895 pink; 161 blue;
    293 yellow
Paterna Stranded Wool (Yarn)
    six skeins: 263 cream
Embroidery frame

FIG 54 Embroidery for chairs

From the plastic canvas, for the table cut two pieces 56 x 34 bars, two legs 44 x 22 bars and two legs 28 x 22 bars, two stay pieces 43 x 4 bars and two pieces 43 x 3 bars.

For each carver chair, cut two backs 36 x 19 bars, four arms 22 x 15 bars, one leg piece 17 x 14 bars and two seats 17 x 15 bars. For each dining chair, cut two backs 36 x 15 bars, three legs 15 x 14 bars and two seats 15 x 15 bars.

For the carpet, cut one piece 113 x 77 bars.

Use twelve strands of stranded cotton (floss) and pearl cotton singly. Embroider the furniture pieces in tent stitch following the charts, noting that some bars are left uncovered for joining to other sections later. Cut away the surplus plastic canvas, taking care to leave one bar beside the embroidery. Overcast the inner sections marked with a cross.

Frame up the cotton canvas and work four chair seats 1³⁄₈in (35mm) square and two 1⁵⁄₈in (40mm) square, using six strands of cotton (floss), alternating cream, green and pink. Embroider the carpet in cross stitch following the chart. Edge stitch in green pearl cotton.

TO MAKE UP THE DINING CHAIRS

Stitch the lower chair seat to the lower uncovered bar of the inner chair back. Stitch the back edge of the upper seat to the upper uncovered bar of the inner back. The other three edges will be left free for the upholstered seat to be inserted later.

Place the three leg sections in position and stitch to the underseat. Join the front corners.

Place the outer back in position, right side outside, and overcast to join to the inner back round the two inner edges, across the top, and down the sides. Three layers will be joined on the leg section. Overcast the remaining uncovered edges.

Take the upholstered seat embroidery from the frame and cut between the pieces, trimming the spare canvas to ½in (13mm) around each piece. Cut four squares of card 1³⁄₈in (35mm) square. Cut three squares of wadding for each

FIG 55 Dining room chairs

brown

(above) Dining room chairs and (below) Dining room table

seat, one the size of the seat aperture, one slightly smaller and one smaller still.

Place the embroidery right side down. Place the wadding on top in order of size, largest first, and place the card over this. Fold the turnings over the card and glue lightly in place. Try the embroidery in the chair seat to make sure it fits. Adjust if necessary and re-glue the turnings. Place in the chair seat, padding the seat space if necessary to give a rounded effect. Overcast the three edges to join the upper seat.

TO MAKE UP THE CARVER CHAIRS

Assemble the seats to the inner back as for the dining chairs. Attach the underseat to the lower edge of the inner arms and front legs. Join the front and back corners. Join the outer arm section to the outer back and overcast the front edges of the arm sections. Place the inner section inside the outer and overcast together all edges EXCEPT the upper seat and front legs. With two strands only in the needle, overcast the front leg corners to hold the two sections together.

Insert the upholstery as for the dining chairs.

TO MAKE UP THE TABLE

Overcast the long edges of the stay pieces together to form an open-ended box shape, overcasting the ends at the same time.

Place the wrong side of one long leg section against the right side of the undertable, matching up the uncovered bars and overcast to join. Repeat with the other long section and then join the short leg sections in the same way.

Overcast the legs together at each corner. Overcast the lower short ends. Using two strands, overcast the stay section to the centre of each side leg section. Place the table top over the under section and overcast all round to join.

FIG 56 Stitching stay to legs

	green
	cream
	pink
	yellow
	blue

Dining room carpet

– 7 –
Dolls' House
Drawing Room Furniture

Chairs and Sofa

This classic drawing room set of sofa and chairs is based on furniture made by Sheraton. The upholstery is embroidered in a stripe design which was very popular in the late-eighteenth century. The main sections are made from two layers of plastic canvas which gives excellent stability. The upholstery at the back and sides is sandwiched between the layers of plastic canvas and the seat pad rests on top.

The materials are sufficient for one sofa, two chairs and the carpet.

MATERIALS

Two 14 x 11in (355 x 280mm) sheets plastic canvas, 10 bars per inch (25mm)

10 x 17in (250 x 430mm) cotton canvas, 18 threads per inch (25mm)

9in (230mm) square of 2oz (50g) Terylene wadding

10 x 8in (250 x 200mm) 1mm card

Clear adhesive or Copydex

Anchor Stranded Cotton (floss)
　14 skeins: 360 brown
　eight skeins: 387 beige
　four skeins: 20 red
　three skeins: 127 navy

Paterna Stranded Wool (Yarn)
　two skeins each of: 570 navy; 444 beige; 950 red
　one skein each of: 834 orange; 554 blue

Embroidery frame

From the plastic canvas, for the sofa cut two backs 60 x 29 bars, four arms 24 x 18 bars, two upper arms 20 x 3 bars, two seats 55 x 18 bars, one front 60 x 22 bars and one front facing 54 x 11 bars.

For each chair, cut two backs 28 x 24 bars, one front 22 x 24 bars, four arms 24 x 18 bars, two seats 19 x 18 bars, four upper arms 20 x 3 bars, and four inside legs 8 x 3 bars.

From the cotton canvas, cut one piece 10 x 7in (250 x 175mm) for the carpet, the remainder is for the upholstery.

From the 1mm card, cut 12 pieces 1½ x 1⅛in (37 x 30mm), two pieces 1⅞ x 1¾in (47 x 40mm), one piece 5¼ x 1¾in (132 x 45mm) and one piece 5¾ x 1⅞in (145 x 47mm).

Use twelve strands of cotton (floss) on the plastic canvas, six for the upholstery. Use a single strand of wool (yarn) for the embroidery of the carpet, two for the edge stitch.

Embroider the plastic-canvas furniture sections following the charts, noting that the outer back sections are not cut away above the seat. These should be covered with lines of sloping satin stitch in beige stranded cotton (floss).

The front leg section of the sofa is made in double thickness plastic canvas, to give strength to the inner legs. Place the front leg facing behind the front section and work the tent stitch across the front and legs through both layers.

Cut away the surplus plastic canvas, taking care to leave one bar beside the embroidery, and trim off the spikes. Overcast the inner sections which are marked with a cross.

TO MAKE UP THE CHAIRS AND SOFA

Make up the inner section first by joining the lower seat to the lower edge of the back cross bar. Join the upper seat to the upper edge. Join the inner arm sections to the inner vertical bars. Join the lower seat edges to the lower edge of the side cross bar.

Next join the outer arm sections to the outer

FIG 57 Assembly of chair or sofa

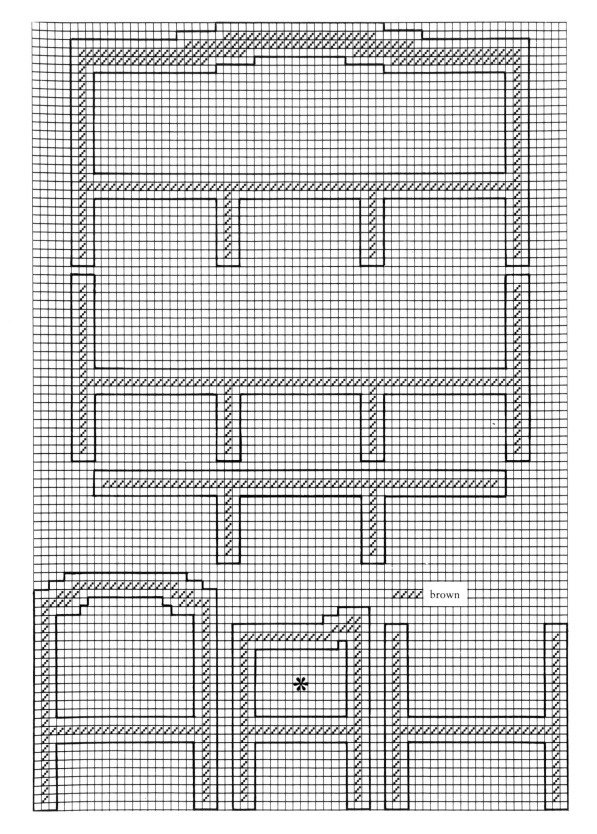

brown

Drawing room furniture

vertical bars of the inner chair back.

Stitch the front cross bar in place along the upper and lower edges of the seat, and at the sides. Next stitch the four small leg sections in place to complete the legs. Leave the upper arm section to one side until the upholstery is ready.

THE UPHOLSTERY

Preparing the cotton canvas: It is ESSENTIAL to work on a frame, as the sloping stitches tend to distort the fabric. As it is very important to keep the stripes running straight take the following steps to ensure this:

Take care to mount the canvas exactly square in the frame.

Work the satin stitch in the same way as half cross, to give a short sloping stitch on the back rather than a long stitch.

Do not work at too tight a tension.

Mark out each section to be embroidered for the furniture with a line of tacking (basting) stitches or with a vanishing pencil, allowing at least 1in (25mm) between them. Mark the back and side sections just a little larger than the area which will show, as no turnings are needed.

For the seat sections, you will need to add turnings because this embroidery will be folded over card to form the cushion. Mark at least 1/4in (6mm) extra all round than the actual size of the card to allow for this. Following the pattern below, and using stranded cotton (floss), work the small sections first, looking out for any sign of the fabric beginning to distort. If it does, work the dark stripes on the two larger pieces in reverse tent stitch, to balance the pull on the fabric. Leave on the frame until required, to avoid any possible relaxation of the canvas.

When ready to proceed remove the embroidered canvas from the frame. Cut between the sections leaving very little extra round the small arm and back sections. Leave more allowance for turning over card on the seat sections.

Take the twelve pieces of card for the arms and check them in position. They should fit snugly inside each arm cavity. Trim the embroidery to fit the card. This should be along the outer edge of the blue stripes.

Cut three pieces of wadding, the first the size of the aperture, the second slightly smaller, the third smaller still. Place these centrally over the card in order of size, smallest first. There should be a narrow width of card showing all round for gluing. Spread glue all round this edge, place the embroidery over it and press in place. Check that the stripes lie exactly in line with the edge, before allowing to bond.

Cover the card for the back of the chairs and sofa in the same way, having first checked that the card is the correct size. It should be a little larger than the aperture.

Cover the card for the chair seats with the embroidery. There needs to be very little underlap of the embroidery on the back and side edges, but a good underlap on the front, as this will be visible.

FITTING THE UPHOLSTERY

Slip the embroidery into the arm section, making sure the stripes are vertical. Place the upper arms in position and stitch in place. The rear end of the arm is joined to the back through the bar next to the top edge.

Glue the inner back embroidery in position behind the inner back plastic canvas, taking great care to keep the stripes vertical. Spread glue over the back of this section, place the outer chair back over it and hold firmly until bonded. Overcast across the top edge to join. Using two strands of cotton (floss) overcast the outer corners to hold them closely together.

Spread glue on the wrong side of the padded seat, close to the edge. Hold in position on the seat until bonded.

Upholstery

The Carpet

The carpet is taken from an Iranian design from Kusack. It keeps the original lines of the design, but has of necessity been very much simplified.

Mark the centre thread of the cotton canvas for the carpet in both directions. This may be done with a fine permanent black felt-tip pen. Frame up the canvas and work the embroidery in tent stitch following the chart, using stranded wool (yarn). The chart shows one quarter of the design. Start with the central medallion, then stitch the main pattern lines before filling in the background.

For clarity, the background is left blank on the chart. The central area is filled in with navy, the next area with red and the outer with navy.

Remove the embroidery from the frame and stretch as necessary or press lightly under a damp cloth from the wrong side. Trim the turnings to about ½in (13mm), and then trim the corners leaving four threads of canvas. Work edge stitch all round the carpet using the cotton canvas technique (see Chapter 12).

Drawing room carpet

– 8 –
Dolls' House Bedroom Furniture

THIS bedroom set is based on a traditional furniture design by Sheraton, made in satinwood and inlaid with mahogany and other woods. Sheraton's furniture was designed for large houses, and therefore these $1/12$ scale models are relatively big. If you are making them for an existing dolls' house it is important to check the size of the rooms first. The wardrobe, for example, is 6in (150mm) tall and $5\frac{1}{4}$in (133mm) wide, but it could be made narrower without losing authenticity.

The furniture has been stitched in light colours to suggest a light wood. The terms light, medium and mahogany are used for the three shades of stranded cotton (floss). Twelve strands of cotton (floss) are used throughout unless otherwise stated. The main embroidery is worked with six strands of light and six strands of medium in the needle and is called the main colour. This gives a slightly mottled, woody appearance to the embroidery. Use two strands of wool (yarn) throughout.

The wardrobe and dressing table are made with 10-bar plastic canvas with an inner shell of ultra-stiff 7-bar canvas to give extra rigidity.

Dressing table, wardrobe, occasional table, bed, rug and carpet

The Wardrobe

In the wardrobe, extra support is given by the drawer dividers and the inner door frame, which help to keep it in shape. A balsa wood frame glued inside the door frame gives it extra rigidity.

MATERIALS

One 14 x 11in (355 x 280mm) sheet of plastic canvas, 10 bars per inch (25mm)

One 12 x 11in (300 x 280mm) sheet ultra-stiff plastic canvas, 7 bars per inch (25mm)

27 x 9in (690 x 230mm) lining fabric

23 x 7in (585 x 175mm) 1mm card

1/4 x 1/4 x 20in (5 x 5 x 510mm) balsa wood (optional)

6in (150mm) 3mm diameter dowelling

3/8in (10mm) stitch-in Velcro

8 gold buttons or brass paper fasteners

Clear adhesive

Anchor Stranded Cotton (floss)
ten skeins each of: 372 light oak; 373 medium oak
six skeins: 358 mahogany

Paterna Stranded Wool (Yarn)
two skeins: 444 beige

From the 10-bar plastic canvas for the outer wardrobe, cut two sides 65 x 20 bars, one top 52 x 20 bars, one back 61 x 52 bars, one facing 52 x 5 bars, two doors 35 x 26 bars, one inner door frame 49 x 33 bars.

For the small drawers, cut two fronts 26 x 6 bars, two bases 23 x 18 bars, four sides 23 x 4 bars and four sides 18 x 4 bars. For the middle drawer cut one front 52 x 7 bars, one base 48 x 18 bars, two sides 48 x 6 bars and two sides 18 x 6 bars. For the large drawer, cut one front 52 x 8 bars, one base 48 x 18 bars, two sides 48 x 7 bars and two sides 18 x 7 bars.

From the 7-bar ultra-stiff plastic canvas, cut one back 40 x 33 bars, two sides 40 x 12 bars, five top and drawer supports 33 x 12 bars, one divider 12 x 4 bars and six rail supports 5 x 5 bars.

From the 1mm card, cut one back 5⅞ x 5in (150 x 128mm), for the cupboard one piece 4¾ x 3⅛in (120 x 80mm), two pieces 3⅛ x 1½in (80 x 38mm), two pieces 4¾ x 1½in (120 x 38mm) and two pieces 3¼ x 2⁵⁄₁₆in (83 x 58mm), for the drawers cut two pieces 2⅛ x 1½in (54 x 38mm) and two pieces 4½ x 1½in (114 x 38mm).

Embroider the doors following the charts. Leaving the hinge edge uncovered work edge stitch around three sides. Work the drawer fronts following the charts. Cover the drawer sides and base with tent stitch using six strands of medium.

Cover the strip for the facing (52 x 5 bars) with lines of tent stitch, alternating mahogany and light. Work similar lines, three stitches deep, across the top edge of the sides (65 x 20). Leave one bar uncovered below this and cover the remaining area with tent stitch in the main colour. Cover the top with tent stitch in the main colour.

For the door frame, work a rectangle of tent stitch next to the outer edge of the inner door frame (49 x 33), and two lines down the centre bars in the main colour. Very carefully cut out the two uncovered areas leaving one bar beside the embroidery. Trim off the spikes and overcast these edges. Stitch the hooked part of the Velcro centrally on the divider.

LINING THE WARDROBE

Using the card as a guide, cut out the fabric for the lining, allowing 5/8in (15mm) extra all round for turnings. Cover each piece of card with fabric. Slipstitch the larger piece of lined card to the 10-bar plastic canvas for the wardrobe back, and place on one side. There should be room at the edges for the needle to pass through when joining the sections.

Attach the door knobs in position. Glue the door lining in place. Stitch the looped part of the Velcro on the edge of the door behind the knobs.

Wardrobe frame and drawer fronts

light oak
medium oak
mahogany

Slipstitch the remaining five pieces of lining to the appropriate plastic canvas to form the interior of the cupboard.

Cut out the centre intersection of the six rail supports (5 x 5). Place three together and overcast to hold together. Repeat with the other three pieces. Glue one rail support to each side lining section, about ½in (13mm) from the top.

TO MAKE UP THE WARDROBE

For the inner shell, using two strands of beige wool (yarn), join the shelves to the sides, starting with the lowest and stitching the divider to the centre of the third and fourth shelves as you do so. Stitch the top and back in place.

Cut the balsa wood into suitably-sized pieces to make a frame the size of the embroidered

Wardrobe door

3 bars
4 bars
5 bars
2 bars

FIG 58 Inner shelves to shell

one. Glue together. Slip the balsa wood section inside the cupboard.

Place the door frame in position and stitch all round. As 10-bar plastic canvas is being joined to 7-bar canvas it will be necessary to work

FIG 59 Door frame

FIG 60 Assembly of outer wardrobe

FIG 61 Drawers

more than one stitch into some holes of the 7-bar canvas. Glue the balsa wood to the back of the frame section. Overcast the remaining uncovered edges.

For the outer shell, overcast the two side sections to the top along the uncovered bars (A). As these stitches form part of the embroidery take care to make them look like tent stitch on the right side.

Overcast the top facing in place (B). Stitch the doors in position. Join the back in place and overcast the remaining edges.

Slip the inner shell inside the outer and glue or catchstitch in place.

For the drawers, attach the knobs in position on the drawer fronts. Assemble the drawers and overcast the top edges. Check the drawers and fronts in position in the wardrobe. The overlap at the centre between the small drawers should be less than that on the outer edge. Decide on exact placement and glue the fronts in place to complete the wardrobe.

The Bed

This bed, complete with mattress and bedlinen, is the size of a double bed but it can be made narrower to suit the size of your dolls' house. The finished size is 4³/4in (120mm) wide and 6¹/2in (165mm) long. If the bed is to fit an existing room, cut the plastic canvas and make a mock-up to check for size.

The mattress is made separately as this allows the sheets and bedspread to be tucked in, like a real bed. The materials given are for the bed and bedding.

MATERIALS

13 x 8in (330 x 200mm) plastic canvas, 7 bars per inch (25mm)

13 x 11in (330 x 280mm) plastic canvas, 10 bars per inch (25mm)

16 x 8in (415 x 200mm) evenweave linen, 18 threads per inch (25mm)

9 x 7¹/4in (230 x 185mm) satin

Anchor Stranded Cotton (floss)

eight skeins: 372 light oak
four skeins: 358 mahogany
one skein: 373 medium oak

Anchor Pearl Cotton No 5
two skeins: 386 cream
one skein each of: 08 light peach; 10 peach

Paterna Stranded Wool (Yarn)
three skeins each of: 263 cream, 444 beige

Wardrobe, occasional table and rug

From the 7-bar plastic canvas, cut one head-board 34 x 25 bars, one footboard 34 x 17 bars, two sides 44 x 9 bars and one base 44 x 34 bars.

From the 10-bar plastic canvas, cut one head-board 51 x 37 bars, one footboard 51 x 25 bars, and for the mattress a top and base 63 x 49 bars each, two sides 63 x 6 bars and two ends 49 x 6 bars.

From the evenweave linen, cut one cover 8 x 8½in (200 x 215mm), four pillow pieces 3½ x 2½in (90 x 60mm) and four cushion pieces 2in (50mm) square.

Use the beige wool (yarn) for the embroidery on the 7-bar plastic canvas, omitting the bed base. Use two strands of the cream wool (yarn) for the mattress.

For the bed inner footboard, cover the 7-bar plastic canvas (34 x 17) with lines of satin and tent stitch, leaving the sixth bar from the base uncovered, for the placement of the bed base. Working from the chart, embroider the 10-bar plastic canvas (51 x 25). Starting at the top edge, embroider the headboard (51 x 37) in the same way. Next work five rows of tent stitch, leave one bar uncovered and complete with six rows of tent stitch. Cover the outer headboard (34 x 25) with rows of satin and tent stitch.

For the bed sides, work two rows of tent stitch down each short edge, and across the top edge. Cut away the uncovered plastic canvas, taking care to leave one bar beside the embroidery. Overcast along the upper edges.

For the mattress, cover the top and four sides with lines of alternating satin and tent stitch. There is no need to embroider the base. Overcast the six pieces into a box shape.

TO MAKE UP THE BED

Join the inner head and footboards to the bed base along the uncovered bar of plastic canvas. Overcast the lower edge of the bed sides to the base. Place the head and footboards in place to the wrong side of the inner pieces and overcast round the upper and side edges to join them, attaching the legs as you do so. Overcast the lower edge of the footboard and legs.

THE BEDDING

For the cover, using light peach work four-sided edge stitch on the linen to give a rectangle 6 x 4½in (150 x 112mm). Fill in the remaining areas with four-sided and stem stitch.

Work the pillows and cushions in the same way as the cradle quilt in Chapter 1, omitting the stem stitch if preferred.

For the valence, fold over a ½in (12mm) turning all round the fabric and tack (baste) in place. Secure with a decorative stitch such as stem stitch.

FIG 63 Bedspread

FIG 62 Construction of bed

The Occasional Table

MATERIALS

5 x 8in (125 x 200mm) plastic canvas, 10 bars per inch (25mm)
Anchor Stranded Cotton (floss)
    two skeins each of: 372 light oak; 373 medium oak
    one skein each of: 358 mahogany; 315 light mahogany

From the plastic canvas, cut a top and under table 26 x 26 bars and four legs 14 x 14 bars.

Embroider the table top following the chart. Work four squares of tent stitch next to the edge of the under table. Cover the four legs with tent stitch. Stitch the legs to the under table along the bar next to the tent stitch. Join the corners and overcast around the base. Overcast the table top in position.

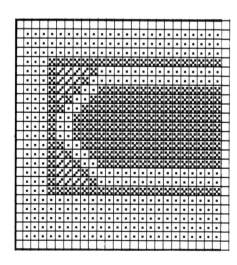

Bed end

The Dressing Table

6in (150mm) square of ultra-stiff plastic canvas, 7 bars per inch (25mm)

12 x 10in (300 x 250mm) plastic canvas, 10 bars per inch (25mm)

Two gold buttons or brass paper fasteners

2⁷⁄₈ x 1³⁄₄in (73 x 44mm) mirror

Clear adhesive or Copydex

Anchor Stranded Cotton (floss)
  six skeins each of: 372 light oak; 373 medium oak
  one skein: 358 mahogany

From the 7-bar plastic canvas, cut one back 26 x 10 bars, one top 26 x 9 bars, one shelf support 26 x 9 bars, two sides 15 x 9 bars and one divider 4 x 8 bars.

From the 10-bar plastic canvas, cut one top 41 x 15 bars, two sides 24 x 15 bars, one back 41 x 22 bars and two mirror pieces 33 x 22 bars. For the drawers, cut two fronts 20 x 6 bars, two bases 17 x 12 bars, four sides 17 x 4 bars and four 12 x 4 bars.

For the inner shell, take the piece of 7-bar plastic canvas for the back and work four rows of 24 tent stitches wide along the base, leaving the top five bars uncovered for the drawer placement. Work nine rows of tent stitch across the base of the sides.

Take the 10-bar plastic canvas pieces and cover the top and sides with tent stitch. Embroider the back, leaving uncovered the top six bars of the last four bars at each end, for the shaped corners.

Work the drawer fronts as in the chart. Attach a knob to the centre of each. Cover the drawer sections with tent stitch using six strands of medium. Join the drawer sections into a box shape. Glue the drawer fronts in position.

For the mirror frame front, work a rectangle of tent stitch in mahogany over the bar next to the outer edge. Inside this stitching work a rectangle in light. Carefully cut out the inner uncovered area, leaving one bar beside the embroidery. Overcast this edge in medium. Cover the mirror back with lines of tent stitch leaving the sixth bar from the lower edge uncovered.

TO MAKE UP THE DRESSING TABLE

Stitch one edge of the divider (4 x 8) to the centre of the shelf. Stitch the shelf to the sides

(top left) Occasional table   (top right) Drawer for dressing table
(below left) Back of dressing table   (below right) Stool

Legend:
light oak
medium oak
light mahogany
mahogany
light/medium oak

Bed, dressing table, stool, carpet and rug

and back, along the bar above the tent stitching, attaching the back of the divider at the same time. Overcast the front edges.

Trim away the uncovered plastic canvas at the top corners of the back section, taking care to leave one bar beside the stitching. Join the table top to the back taking the stitching through the uncovered bar, and overcasting the short vertical edges as you do so. Place the sides in position and stitch to the top and back.

Place the mirror back over the back edge,

matching up the uncovered bars and overcast to join. Place the mirror front in position and overcast round two sides. Insert the mirror glass and complete the stitching. Overcast the remaining uncovered edges.

Spread adhesive evenly over the back of the inner shell, sides and back and along the overcasting at the top edge. Place this inside the outer section and hold together with clothes pegs or clips until bonded.

FIG 64 Dressing table

The Stool

MATERIALS

7 x 3in (175 x 75mm) plastic canvas, 10 bars per inch (25mm)

3½ x 2½in (90 x 63mm) evenweave linen, 18 threads per inch (25mm)

3½ x 2½in (90 x 63mm) contrasting fabric for lining the seat

2 x 1¼in (50 x 32mm) piece of thin card

Oddments of wadding

Clear adhesive or Copydex

Anchor Stranded Cotton (floss)
two skeins each of: 372 light oak; 373 medium oak
one skein: 358 mahogany

Anchor Pearl Cotton No 5
one skein: 386 cream

From the plastic canvas, cut four sides 14 x 14 bars, two sides 22 x 5 bars, and two tops 22 x 14 bars.

Use twelve strands of cotton throughout. Embroider the sides following the charts. Cut out the aperture of one seat top and overcast the inner edge. Join the long sides to the other top section, then join the inner sides along the bar above the embroidery, making a shallow box shape. Place the outer sides in position and stitch down the sides and across the base, so joining the sections.

Work a 2⅜ x 1½in (60 x 37mm) area of four-sided stitch in the centre of the evenweave linen. Tack (baste) the contrasting fabric behind it, using small stitches.

Place the embroidery over the card, gluing the turnings to the back, taking care that the lines of stitching are true with the edges, stuffing with wadding to give a rounded shape. Place the frame in position and overcast to join along two sides. Insert the embroidery and complete the stitching, stuffing with wadding before completing.

The Carpet

MATERIALS

One 14 x 11in (355 x 280mm) sheet of plastic canvas, 10 bars per inch (25mm)

Paterna Stranded Wool (Yarn)
12 skeins: 756 cream

Using two strands of wool (yarn) throughout, work a border of satin stitch over three bars then a rectangle of tent stitch inside the satin stitch. Repeat the satin stitch and tent stitch borders once. Work a rectangle of satin stitch over two bars.

Fill in the central area with Milanese stitch (see Chapter 12).

The Rug

MATERIALS

One piece 77 x 53 bars of plastic canvas, 14 bars per inch (25mm)

Anchor Stranded Cotton (floss)
one skein each of: 860 green; 883 rust; 313 yellow; 160 blue; 275 cream

Use three strands of cotton (floss) throughout.

This pattern is worked in the same way as the border of the dining room carpet in Chapter 6. The size of the rug may be varied to suit the room setting.

– 9 –
Miniature Pictures

*T*HESE decoratively-stitched pictures are quick to sew and make ideal small projects. The floral pictures are stitched in freehand embroidery while the cottage picture is counted-thread embroidery.

The cross stitch cottage picture is worked on Aida fabric with 22 threads to the inch (25mm). Good light is essential for counted-thread embroidery and a magnifier certainly helps. Working from a chart needs concentration but the resulting embroidery is attractive. Be warned, it rapidly becomes addictive.

In complete contrast is the freer, more textured type of embroidery used in the four little flower pictures and the two miniatures. Here results can be achieved relatively quickly, without the eye strain of counting the threads. The textured stitches and variation in the cotton colours make the pictures particularly interesting.

Pulled-fabric flower pictures and cottage sampler

Pulled-fabric Flower Pictures

These four little pulled-fabric flower pictures have been worked on a synthetic voile-type fabric, intended for curtains. Using only straight stitches, French knots and a little seeding, they are worked in stranded cotton (floss).

Working stitches to a tight tension on loosely-woven fabric pulls the fabric into holes. The looser the weave of the fabric, the larger the holes become. Straight stitches worked radially around a central hole give a pretty flower shape. When mixed with French knots a lively variation in texture is achieved.

SPRING IN THE GARDEN

This colourful picture is adapted from a photograph taken from my studio window in spring. The sample was worked by eye straight from the photograph. The areas of green were reduced, and the two clumps of primula in the foreground enlarged slightly to give more colour. The bergenia is really a mauvey-pink colour which is difficult to match, so I have mixed mauve and pink threads to achieve the right tone for the French knots.

MATERIALS

6in (150mm) square of synthetic voile
5¼in (135mm) square picture frame
4in (100mm) diameter circle 1mm card
Greetings card with a 3in (75mm) diameter
    aperture for the inner mount
7in (178mm) square of polyester crepe in a dark
    colour
2mm card to fit picture frame, with a 3½in
    (90mm) diameter aperture cut from centre
15 x 3in (380 x 75mm) wadding
Crochet cotton for lacing
Vanishing pencil
Clear adhesive
Anchor Stranded Cotton (floss)
    one skein or small amounts of: 41 salmon;
    75 pink; 118 iris; 108 mauve; 302 yellow;
    268 deep grass green; 876 green; 817 bright
    grass green; 259 light grass green; 376 beige;
    359 brown; 856 olive brown
4in (100mm) embroidery hoop

NOTE: A circular picture frame would be equally suitable, as shown in the alternative version of *Spring in the Woods*, in which case the 2mm card mount is not needed.

The embroidery may be worked by eye, straight onto the fabric, adapting the areas of stitching as you go, for the desired effect. If you find a guide is really necessary, the outline may be transferred to the fabric as follows:

FIG 65 Pulled-work embroidery in progress

Make a tracing of the design onto tissue or greaseproof paper. Place the tracing centrally on the fabric and tack into place. Work small running stitches all round the design, using tacking (basting) cotton. Pull the tissue paper away carefully. The tacking (basting) should be removed when no longer needed.

Mark the outer area to be embroidered onto the selected fabric. This should be slightly larger than the card aperture. Mount the fabric, drum tight, centrally in the embroidery hoop, taking care to keep the straight grain running correctly from top to bottom.

Stitch the design in straight stitch and French knots, and work the background in seeding. Remove from the frame and press, if wished, from the wrong side. Use the mount aperture to check that sufficient embroidery has been worked, adding more stitching if necessary.

MOUNTING THE PICTURE

Cut five circles of wadding, one the size of the mount aperture (3in/75mm), the others in decreasing size. Place the embroidery right side down with the five pieces of wadding centrally over it, the largest first, the others in decreasing size. Place the circle of 1mm card centrally on top. Fold the excess fabric over the card and lace the turnings using about two yards or metres of crochet cotton. Fold the surplus fabric to the back and lace round securing the edges with long herringbone stitches (see page 119).

Cut away and discard the two outer sections of the greetings card. Place the square of dark fabric right side down with the aperture of the card centrally over it. Mark the outline with a vanishing pencil. Cut out the centre of the fabric, leaving ½in (13mm) for turning. Snip fabric to the marked line at intervals of about ⅜in (10mm). Spread adhesive all round the opening, and fold the turning to cover the edge. Pull tightly so that the fabric is taut over the edge.

To assemble the picture, place embroidery right side up and apply glue around the edge. Position the fabric-covered mount on top and leave until bonded. Place the 2mm card mount on top and fix into the frame.

SPRING IN THE WOODS

This picture is based on a photograph taken on a walking holiday in America, and is a memento of good times. We were walking in the Blue Ridge Mountains amongst the bare trees and suddenly came upon this tree of blossom outlined against the sky.

Follow the materials and instructions for *Spring in the Garden* using the following colours:

Anchor Stranded Cotton (floss)
one skein each or small amounts of: 153 blue; 300 pale yellow; 253 light green; 843 olive green; 856 olive brown; 905 brown

SUMMER IN WALES

This embroidery is based on a photograph of Bodnant Garden, Clwyd, taken from a calender. The dramatic colours are set off by the sombre colours of the trees, and a shaft of sunlight lights up the middle ground. The sunlit lawn in the foreground gives further contrast.

Follow the materials and instructions for *Spring in the Garden*, using the following colours:

Anchor Stranded Cotton (floss)
one skein each or small amounts of: 41 salmon; 35 deep salmon; 68 raspberry; 108 mauve; 98 purple; 89 cerise; 160 blue; 300 pale yellow; 926 cream; 381 brown; 216 green; 218 dark green; 265 grass green; 846 olive green; 259 light grass green; 843 light olive green; 01 white

SUMMER IN A VASE

This embroidery is adapted from a painting by Renoir. The flowers appear almost three-dimensional, seeming to come out of the canvas. The chief interest is in the deep contrast between the background and the flowers, with the dark shiny vase forming a foil in texture and colour. The colours have a wonderfully soft appearance, merging with one another to give a rich glow.

Follow the materials and instructions for

Spring in the Garden

Summer in a Vase

Spring in the Woods

Summer in Wales

FIG 66 *Tracing of four pictures and the placement of colours*

Spring in the Garden using the following colours:

Anchor Stranded Cotton (floss)
  one skein each or small amounts of:
  19 pink/red; 4146 pale peach; 79 raspberry;
  9575 peach; 352 rust; 303, 305 and 307
  yellow; 382 brown; 921 blue/grey; 926 cream;
  214 and 217 green

The flowers are all worked in straight stitch, some flowers are pulled into holes at the centre, some have centres filled with stitches, and the poppies are worked leaving a central area for the French knots.

Seeding is used for the background as this is a flat stitch and ensures that the flowers stand out.

In the pictures above, the numbers indicate where the different colours go.

Dolls' House Miniatures

Both of these tiny pictures are worked in stranded cotton (floss) on voile, using the same technique as in the previous pictures. One is the well-known Van Gogh Sunflowers, *the other is based on* Hollyhocks and other Flowers in a Vase *by Jan Van Huijsum. Frames suitable for doll's house pictures may be purchased from specialist shops. The materials given are sufficient for both embroideries.*

MATERIALS

4 x 3½in (100 x 90mm) each of light and black lightweight voile
1mm card
Inner mount fabric
Wadding
Picture frames
Crochet cotton for lacing
Anchor Stranded Cotton (floss)
Sunflowers: a small amount each of: 326 orange; 868 pink/peach; 889 brown; 5975 red/rust; 366 cream
Hollyhocks: a small amount each of: 868 pink/peach; 24 pink; 161 blue; 117 pale blue; 22 dark red; 46 red; 214 light green; 218 dark green; 02 white
4in (100mm) embroidery hoop

Measure the aperture of the picture frame and mark this area onto the fabric with a line of tacking (basting). Work the embroidery as for the four circular flower pictures.

See Chapter 11 for mounting the pictures. To finish, make a small thread loop near the top of the larger piece of card, for hanging. Place the embroidery in the frame aperture and glue the card on top to hold it in place.

FIG 67 *Thread loop for hanging*

Dolls' house miniature pictures and cottage sampler

Cottage Picture

The technique for this picture is in complete contrast to the pulled work of the other pictures. The formal cross stitches are counted carefully, to ensure accuracy.

Miniature pictures make attractive gifts or cards for friends. Stitched to mark a special occasion such as the birth of a baby, a wedding or a christening, they give a really personal touch. A cross stitch sampler of a friend's house would make a very special present.

MATERIALS
MATERIALS

6 x 5in (150 x 130mm) white Aida, 22 threads per
  inch (25mm)
6 x 5in (150 x 130mm) black velvet
6 x 5in (150 x 130mm) lightweight black fabric
5 x 3¾in (130 x 95mm) 2mm card
4¼ x 3⅛in (105 x 75mm) 1mm card
Anchor Stranded Cotton (floss)
  one skein each or small amounts of: 403 black;
  400 charcoal; 883 brown; 216 green; 131 blue;
  33 pink; 305 yellow; 373 beige; 848 light
  blue/green; 47 red
Embroidery frame

Work the main design in cross stitch using two strands of cotton (floss). Work the roof in brick stitch using one strand each of black, charcoal and brown stranded cotton (floss) in the needle. Outline the post box mouth in black back stitch.

Mount the embroidery over card using herringbone stitch. Cut a piece of 2mm card to the size required. This should be at least 1in (25mm) bigger than the embroidery, allowing a reasonable border to show all round. Cut a piece of 1mm card very slightly smaller.

Cover the larger card with velvet or similar fabric. Cover the smaller card with lightweight fabric, having first stitched on rings for hanging if required. Glue the lined card to the back of the velvet-covered card, covering the raw edges. Spread glue evenly on the back of the embroidery and place centrally over the velvet-covered board. Take great care that it is central. Place a weight on top and allow to bond.

FRAMING

If there is a space between the embroidery and the depth of the frame rebate, cut a piece of backing card which is slightly smaller than the back of the frame, to fill the gap. Place the embroidery in the frame aperture and glue the card over it to hold it in place.

Cottage picture

	black		green
▨		◤	

	yellow		blue
▥		+	

	blue/green		beige
⊤		▨	

	brown		pink
Y		·	

	charcoal		red
▢		▨	

– 10 –
Festive Embroidery

CHRISTMAS is a time of tradition, the gathering of family and friends and for bringing out favourite decorations. All the decorations given here should last for many years. The ribbon and other yarns will keep their sheen, and as they are easily washable will stay looking new for future generations.

Most of the decorations could be adapted in other ways, made on a different-sized plastic canvas, or worked on natural fabrics such as Aida. Cream Aida may become slightly patchy unless washed with care. A cream evenweave linen could also be used and this would wash and wear for years, given the chance.

The trees in the border design may be readily altered in height and width, and the spacing varied. Try to keep an even number of bars between them so that the pointed star may be placed centrally.

Fruit bowl, sweets basket, napkin rings, coasters and placemat

Table Centre or Placemat

A small Christmas plant or a bowl of fruit looks very effective placed on this mat, on the table or sideboard. The mat could be easily altered in size and shape. To make a long runner, it could be worked with just one central pattern.

As plastic canvas from the main manufacturers varies slightly in sheet size, it is recommended that the outer border of double cross stitch be worked first in order to define the outline of the design. The mesh may then be trimmed as necessary.

· · · · · red cross		✕✕✕✕✕ green cross	▨▨▨▨ green satin
▨▨▨▨ gold tent		✦✦✦✦ green/gold double cross	
▪▪▪▪ gold cross			

Christmas tablemat

MATERIALS

One sheet of plastic canvas, 10 bars per inch
  (25mm)
14⅞ x 11¾in (370 x 300mm) cotton or
  polycotton backing fabric
Anchor Stranded Cotton (floss)
  fifteen skeins: 46 red
  sixteen skeins: 228 green
One ball of Twilleys Goldfingering

Darice plastic canvas measures 137 x 107 bars,
and for this design it will be necessary to trim
off one bar along the length and width of the

mesh. Uniek plastic canvas measures 141 x 111
bars, and it will be necessary to trim off five bars
in both directions. Use the full six strands of
cotton (floss), except for the satin stitch squares,
for which twelve strands will be needed. The
gold thread is used singly. The pointed stars (see
page 113) and those on the main tree are
worked on top of the small cross stitch.

Complete the embroidery following the
chart. Trim the mesh as necessary. Edge stitch
all round in red. Fold under and tack (baste) the
turnings on the backing and slipstitch in place
using three strands of red.

Coasters

For these you can work four identical coasters, or vary each one slightly as in the examples. Silver yarn, or one of the other colours of goldfingering could be used as alternatives to gold.

MATERIALS

Four pieces of plastic canvas, 10 bars per inch (25mm), 34 bars square
Four 4⅝in (115mm) squares of cotton or polycotton backing fabric
Anchor Stranded Cotton (floss)
    four skeins each of: 46 red; 228 green
One ball of Twilleys Goldfingering

Use the full six strands of stranded cotton (floss), except for the satin stitch squares, for which twelve strands will be needed. Use the gold thread singly. The stars on the trees are worked on top of the small cross stitch.

On two of the coasters work the double cross stitch in red and gold, the satin stitch in green. On the other two, work the double cross stitch in green and gold, the satin stitch in red.

Work the trees in green with a red background, or the trees in red with a green background, to give individuality to each coaster. Edge stitch in the same colour as the satin stitch.

Fold under and tack (baste) ⅝in (15mm) turnings on the backing. Slipstitch in place using three strands to match the edge stitch.

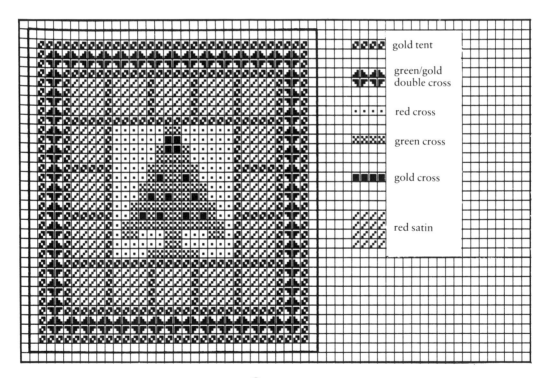

gold tent
green/gold double cross
red cross
green cross
gold cross
red satin

Coasters

Napkin Rings

Both designs complement the pattern of the table mat and each could be varied slightly to personalise them; cross stitch could be used instead of satin stitch, alternate squares could be red and green, the Christmas trees could also have individually coloured lights.

The materials given are sufficient for four napkin rings.

MATERIALS

6in square (150mm) plastic canvas, 10 bars per inch (25mm)
Anchor Stranded Cotton (floss)
  four skeins each of: 46 red; 228 green
12yd (11m) Twilleys Goldfingering

From the plastic canvas, for the napkin rings with the tree design, cut four pieces 54 x 14 bars. For the square-design rings, cut four pieces 56 x 12 bars.

Use the full six strands of the cotton (floss), except for the satin stitch for which twelve strands will be needed. Use the goldfingering thread singly.

For each ring, leave the first and last four or six bars of plastic canvas uncovered and work the chosen design from the chart. Overlap the uncovered ends, matching up the bars and complete the embroidery by stitching through both layers, so joining into a ring. Edge stitch all round in red or green, to finish.

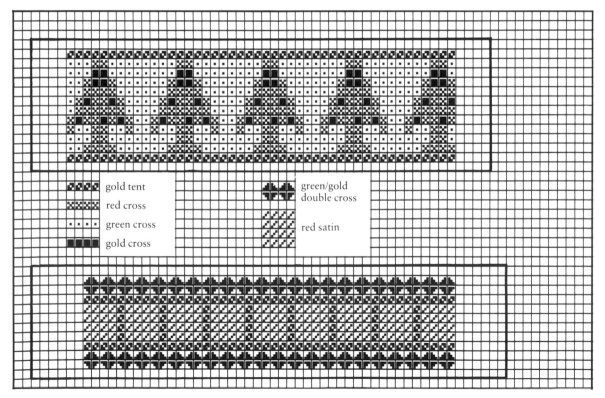

Napkin rings

Fruit Bowl

This decorative bowl is made by slipping an embroidered ring of plastic canvas over an inner bowl lining. The inner bowl is also made of plastic canvas, so it may be removed for separate, more frequent washing.

The embroidered ring could be adapted to make a festive cake band. Measure the circumference of the cake to be covered and make one long strip, allowing an extra couple of inches. Do not join into a ring as it will be overlapped and pinned in place on the cake. The width could be altered by omitting two or more rows of the tent stitch or the double cross stitch.

MATERIALS

11 x 6in (280 x 150mm) plastic canvas, 10 bars per inch (25mm)

18 x 6in (455 x 150mm) ultra-stiff plastic canvas, 7 bars per inch (25mm)

Two 9½in (240mm) diameter plastic-canvas circles

18 x 36in (455 x 900mm) cotton or polycotton lining fabric

7in (175mm) square of card

12 x 15in (300 x 375mm) 2oz wadding

Anchor Stranded Cotton (floss)
six skeins each of: 46 red; 228 green

Half a ball of Twilleys Goldfingering

From the 10-bar plastic canvas cut two sides 29 x 105 bars and two backing strips 8 x 29 bars. From the 7-bar plastic canvas, cut one

FIG 68 Backing strip

FIG 69 Overlapped joins

piece 121 x 18 bars and one piece 22 x 18 bars.

Use six strands of cotton (floss) for the embroidery and three strands for sewing the lining fabric. Use the gold thread singly.

Tack (baste) a backing strip to the right short edges of both side pieces of plastic canvas. Leaving the first four bars uncovered, embroider the sides following the chart. When the stitching nears the right edge, tack (baste) the second length of plastic canvas over the backing strip, matching the bars. Continue the embroidery through both layers to join them. When you reach the right-hand backing strip overlap the left edge over it and complete the embroidery through both layers, to join into a ring. Edge stitch each side in gold.

LINING THE BOWL

To prepare the lining fabric, use the length of ultra-stiff canvas as a guide, cut the fabric for the lining on the bias, with each long side the same length as the 7-bar plastic canvas, and

FIG 70 Fabric on the bias

Fruit bowl and napkin rings

adding ¾in (20mm) to each long side for turnings. No seam allowance is needed on the short edges as the fabric will be stretched tightly over the lining plastic canvas, giving a smooth fit.

Fold under ½in (13mm) on each short edge and place them together as shown. When the seam is opened out the straight edges must be in a straight line. Overcast with close stitching using three strands of cotton (floss). Press open.

FIG 74 Seam pressed open

stitches about 1in (25mm) from the long edges, butting the ends rather than overlapping, to avoid bulk.

Place the lining fabric inside the plastic canvas, wrong side against the wadding. Turn about ¾in (20mm) of lining at the upper edge over the canvas to the outside and stitch in place. Take tiny, almost invisible, stitches on the right side, larger ones on the wrong side. Fold the lining on the lower edge under the wadding, so that the fold lies between the two

FIGS 71 and 72 Joining on the bias

FIG 75 Lining the interior

FIG 73 Completed join showing stitches

Join the ultra-stiff canvas into a ring by overlapping four bars and joining firmly with cross stitch through both layers. Cut a strip of wadding to fit inside this and tack, placing the

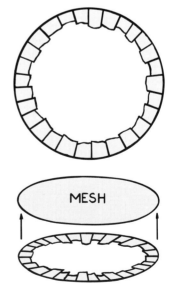

FIGS 76 and 77 Lining the base

	gold satin
	green/gold double cross
	green cross
	red cross
	gold cross

lower bars, leaving room for the needle to pass through when joining the side to the base. Slipstitch in place, taking the stitches over every other intersection of the canvas.

For the base of the bowl, cut a circle from the centre of one plastic-canvas circle, leaving a frame 10 bars wide. This should give a circle of $6^{3}/_{16}$in (160mm) diameter for the base of the lining. The frame may be useful for another project. (As the size of circles may vary according to the manufacturer check carefully that this will be correct before cutting.)

Cut a circle of card slightly smaller than the plastic-canvas circle. The edge should come be-

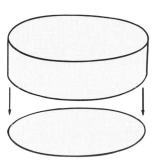

FIG 78 Side to base

tween the outer edge and the first bar. Place the fabric for the base right side down with the card centrally over it. Press the turnings over the card to mark the edges. Remove the card and slipstitch the fabric to the plastic-canvas circle, to form the underside of the base.

Overcast the prepared lined side to the lined base. Place the embroidery in position over the bowl lining. It should be a tight fit, and no stitching should be necessary to join them.

Cut a circle from the centre of the other plastic-canvas circle, one bar smaller than the first. Cover this with wadding and fabric. Slipstitch the turning to the wrong side. Slip inside base to complete the fruit bowl.

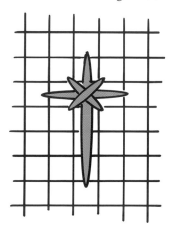

Pointed star stitch

The Sweets Basket

This is designed to fit over a box of mints. No lining is necessary, as the interior is completely covered by the box. The smaller circle listed below is optional. It covers the centre of a box of mints.

MATERIALS

14 x 5in (355 x 125mm) plastic canvas,
10 bars per inch (25mm)
one 5¾in (145mm) and one 3in (75mm)
diameter plastic-canvas circles
Anchor Stranded Cotton (floss)
seven skeins: 46 red
four skeins: 228 green
Half a ball of Twilleys Goldfingering

Sweets basket side and (right) handle

From the plastic canvas, cut one side 16 x 120 and one 16 x 60 bars, two backing strips 8 x 16 bars and one handle 134 x 11 bars. The pointed stars (see page 113) and those on the main tree are worked on top of the completed cross stitch. Use the full six strands of cotton (floss), the gold thread singly.

Leaving the first and last four bars uncovered, embroider the handle following the chart. Between the trees work long tied cross stitch stars over the red cross stitch background. Edge stitch both edges beside the embroidery in gold thread.

Tack (baste) a backing strip to the right short edges of the two side sections. Starting with the longer strip, and leaving the first four bars uncovered, work the embroidery following the chart. Leave a gap in the stitching at the centre of the upper long edge for placing the handle

FIG 79 Overlap

FIG 80 Handle in position

later. This should be at least four bars deep and extend across the 7th and 8th tree pattern. The exact size does not matter, it just needs to be as wide or a little wider than the handle.

When the stitching nears the right edge, tack (baste) the second length of plastic canvas over the backing strip, matching the bars. Embroider through both layers to join them. At the right end leave fifteen or more bars uncovered.

Tack (baste) one end of the handle behind the plastic canvas between the 7th and 8th patterns. Complete the embroidery through both layers.

Overlap the left edge of the side over the backing strip on the right to form a ring, and tack (baste) securely in place. Place the free end of the handle beside the backing strip, underlapping it by four bars, and complete the embroidery, securing the join and the handle.

Embroider the larger circle in satin and tent stitch, alternating the colours, for the base. If using the 3in (75mm) circle, satin stitch in red and green with a gold Rhodes stitch at the centre. Edge stitch all round.

TO MAKE UP THE BASKET

Place the side over the base and stitch all round, either in edge stitch or overcasting. The former is more decorative, but as 10-bar plastic canvas is being joined to the equivalent of 7-bar canvas it would be easier to use overcasting.

– 11 –

Equipment and Basic Techniques

PLASTIC CANVAS

Plastic canvas is available with seven and ten bars to the inch, in sheets measuring approximately 14 x 11in (355 x 280mm), the size varying slightly between different manufacturers. Where a full sheet is specified for the projects this variation has been allowed for. 7-bar plastic canvas is also available in larger sheets and a variety of stiffnesses. Mesh with fourteen bars to the inch (25mm) is available in sheets measuring 11 x 8¼in (280 x 210mm).

Plastic canvas should be cut with scissors to the size specified, counting bars, not holes. Before cutting out the pieces, plan the position of each piece on the canvas to ensure that all the pieces will fit economically. Where edges have been cut, trim off any spikes before starting to stitch, to avoid the cotton or wool (yarn) catching.

Plastic-canvas circles are available, ranging from 3in (75mm) to 12in (300mm) diameter. They are either square-mesh circles where the bars lie at right angles to each other (as used in the Cradle, Chapter 1) or radial circles with the bars radiating from the centre. The circles vary in bar count as well as diameter. They can easily be trimmed to a smaller size if required, and the surplus used for picture frames, see Chapter 9.

Tacking (basting) on plastic canvas should pass between the bars, to avoid damage. The outer bar is normally left unstitched, for overcasting or joining to other pieces later.

Plastic canvas may be washed with care in hand hot water.

COTTON CANVAS

The projects in this book use canvas with 10, 12, 14 or 18 threads per inch (25mm). The number of canvas threads per inch (25mm) will dictate the size of stitch and the thickness of thread used to ensure the canvas is covered.

For all projects, it is better to work on an embroidery frame to avoid distorting the canvas. Allow 1-2in (25-50mm) extra fabric around the design, for attaching to the frame. All stitches on canvas should be worked in two movements. Bring the needle up and pull the cotton or wool (yarn) through the canvas, take it down and pull it through.

EVENWEAVE FABRICS

As the name suggests, evenweave fabrics have the same number of warp and weft threads per inch (25mm). Linen has a plain weave, Aida a special square weave. Neither need to be completely covered with stitches. Care should be taken when washing cream Aida as it may become slightly patchy.

Linda is a very finely-woven fabric used for counted-thread work, such as the Cradle quilt in Chapter 1. Evenweave linen is very hard-wearing and can be washed many times and still last for years.

THE CHARTS

Each square of a chart represents one thread or bar of the background fabric.

WOOL (YARN) AND COTTON

Paterna Stranded Wool (Yarn) is a twisted 3-ply wool (yarn). To separate the strands, hold the end of one strand and gently push the other two down against it to remove them. It is available in 8m skeins or 4oz hanks.

Anchor Stranded Cotton (floss) is a fine thread with a shiny finish, in six separable strands. Separate the strands as for the wool.

Anchor Pearl Cotton No 5 is a twisted thread with a slight sheen. It doesn't have separable threads and is either used singly or doubled.

All care has been taken to record the cotton and wool (yarn) quantities needed with reasonable accuracy, but amounts used by different embroiderers may need adjustment.

SEWING TIPS

For all cottons and wools (yarns), try to keep the tension even when stitching, giving it a slight pull as you work each stitch so that it lies evenly on the surface. When working on plastic canvas, you may prefer to work at a slightly looser tension than usual, allowing the stitches to puff out and give a good cover.

On plastic canvas it is best to work with a maximum 36in (900mm) length of yarn in the needle, except for wide satin stitch, Rhodes and edge stitch when about 72in (1.8m) may be used, to avoid making joins. On cotton canvas 18in (0.5m) or even less should be used except for the stitches mentioned. You will need to untwist the threads from time to time.

STARTING AND FINISHING THREADS

Knot the end of the thread and take it through to the back of the work about 1in (25mm) forward of where you are intending to stitch. Work the first few stitches over the thread on the back and then cut off the knot when it is

reached. After the first row of stitches a new length may be joined in by running it through the back of previous stitching. Finish off by running the thread through the back of the last few stitches.

RIBBON

Some of the projects in this book use very fine 1.5mm Offray ribbon for stitching which gives a lovely rich look to the embroidery. For maximum sheen the ribbon should lie flat on the surface. As you work each stitch, hold the ribbon between finger and thumb and guide it through the canvas to keep it flat. Unthread the needle frequently to untwist the ribbon.

NEEDLES

Blunt-ended tapestry needles should be used for working on canvas and for pulled-thread work. They come in a variety of sizes; size No 22 is best for working on 14 count Aida. No 20 is a good general size for working with stranded cotton (floss) or two strands of wool (yarn). No 18 is needed for working with three strands of wool (yarn).

MAKING BOXES

BOX WITH SEPARATE LID

Place one side of the box against the base, with wrong sides facing and edges matched up, and overcast or edge stitch to join them. Repeat with the other three sides. Stitch the corners. Overcast or edge stitch around the top edge. Make up the lid in the same way as the box. If the box is unlined, assemble with the right side of the base uppermost.

FIG 81 Starting and finishing

FIG 82 Box with lid

BOX WITH ATTACHED LID

Make up the box as above. But only overcast or edge stitch around three sides of the box and the lid. Place the unstitched edges of box and lid together, wrong sides facing, and edge stitch or overcast to join. Work at a medium tension. Tight stitches will prevent the lid from seating properly.

Make a tassel at the centre lid front (see Gold Initial Box, Chapter 4). If the lid does not lie quite flat when the box is complete, dampen a lightweight cloth and place this over the box, with a book on top. This should not be so heavy that it distorts the box.

FIG 83 Box with lid attached

LINING A BOX

Cut the card for lining the box with a craft knife to give a good smooth edge. Use an emery board to smooth the edges if necessary. Ultra-stiff plastic canvas may be substituted for card when lining boxes, to make them washable.

Use the card as a guide to cut the lining fabric, allowing ⅝in (15mm) all round for turnings. A smaller turning would be suitable for small pieces.

For cutting the wadding, use the card as a guide and cut to the same size. If it seems to be too thick it may be carefully separated into two layers.

To cover the card with lining, place the fabric right side down, with the wadding, if using, and the card on top. Spread adhesive evenly around

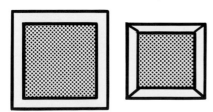

FIG 84 Covering card with fabric

the edge of the card and fold the turning over, holding in position until bonded. Take care to tuck the turnings in away from the edge, so that they will not show when the lining is in place.

FIG 85 Card lining

To insert the lining, glue the longer side linings in place first, followed by the shorter ones, which fit in between, giving the box rigidity. Take great care not to get adhesive on the right side of the fabric. It may not show up right away, but soon develops into a black mark which is not removable.

MAKING A PINCUSHION PAD

The fabric should be cut in a rectangle which will be folded in half and stitched to give a pad a fraction larger than the finished embroidery. This will give a good firm finish to the pincushion.

Fold under and press the seam allowances on the two shorter edges of the fabric. Fold in half lengthways and stitch the sides, catching down the seam allowances as you do so.

Slipstitch the remaining side, stuffing with wool (yarn) offcuts or with Terylene wadding before closing the gap (see Fig 86).

BEDDING FOR THE CRADLE

Mattress Make up as for the pincushion, stuffing with flat layers of Terylene wadding, and slipstitching the opening invisibly.

FIG 86 Pincushion or mattress pad

Pillow Fold the fabric for the pillow in half to mark the centre. Work stem stitch to form a border on one side, making allowance for the turnings when stitched. Make up in the same way as the mattress.

MOUNTING AND FRAMING AN EMBROIDERY

MOUNTING ON CARD

Check that all threads ends are neatly finished off, and press the embroidery from the wrong side. Decide how much fabric you wish to show all round the embroidery as a border, and cut the backing card to this size. If the embroidery is to fit in a frame then the backing card needs to be slightly smaller than the recess.

Cut a piece of wadding the size of the frame aperture. If mounting a circular embroidery which you wish to dome, cut several pieces in decreasing size.

Place the embroidery right side down on a work surface, followed by the wadding in order of size, and place the backing card centrally on top.

Thread the needle with about two yards or metres of strong thread such as crochet cotton. Fold the surplus fabric to the back on the two

FIG 87 Lacing with herringbone stitch

long edges, and lace across to secure them with long herringbone stitches. IT IS IMPORTANT TO CHECK ON THE RIGHT SIDE THAT THE FABRIC GRAIN IS LYING ALONG THE EDGE OF THE CARD. When you reach the right edge pull the thread as taut as possible and fasten off very securely. If the mount is circular work right round.

Repeat the lacing process in the other direction, tucking in the corners of the fabric.

MOUNTING ON FABRIC-COVERED BOARD

This method is used for the Cottage picture, Chapter 9. Mount the embroidery over card using herringbone stitch. Cut a piece of 2mm card to the size required. This should be at least 1in (25mm) bigger than the embroidery, allowing a reasonable border to show all round. Cut a piece of 1mm card very slightly smaller.

FIG 88 Mounting the cottage picture

Cover the larger card with velvet or similar fabric. Cover the smaller card with lightweight fabric, having first stitched on rings for hanging if required. Glue the lined card to the back of the velvet-covered card, covering the raw edges. Spread glue evenly on the back of the embroidery and place centrally over the velvet-covered board. Take great care that it is central. Place a weight on top and allow to bond.

FRAMING

If there is a space between the embroidery and the depth of the frame rebate, cut a piece of backing card which is slightly smaller than the back of the frame, to fill the gap. Place the embroidery in the frame aperture and glue the card over it to hold it in place.

– 12 –
The Stitches

COUNTED-THREAD STITCHES

TENT STITCH

Work from right to left with each stitch passing over one intersection of the canvas. This method makes a long sloping stitch on the back, and gives a good cover. Subsequent rows may be worked from left to right, but take care that the back looks the same. This stitch tends to distort cotton canvas.

FIG 89 Tent stitch

HALF CROSS STITCH

This looks like tent stitch on the front, but has a small straight stitch on the back of the work. Start by working from left to right. It does not give such a good cover as tent stitch, and is not so hard-wearing. However, it takes less yarn and does not distort cotton canvas as does tent stitch.

FIG 90 Half cross stitch

VELVET STITCH

Begin at the lower edge of the space to be covered. This is a cross stitch with an extra stitch which forms a loop. It should be worked from the base upwards. The loop may be formed by holding the thread down. A more even result is obtained by wrapping the thread round a knitting needle or pencil. Hold this just below the line of stitching and leave it in place

until the row is completed. The loops may be cut or not as preferred, on completion.

Work the first stitch of the cross from bottom right to top left and then work another stitch ON TOP OF IT, this time making a loop as shown. Complete the cross, thus tying down the loop. Repeat as required.

FIG 91 Velvet stitch

DOUBLE CROSS STITCH

A diagonal cross stitch over two threads is worked first in wool (yarn), and then a straight cross is worked over it. The straight cross stitch may be in the same cotton or wool (yarn), or in a contrast.

FIG 92 Double cross stitch

SMALL CROSS STITCH

This stitch passes over one intersection.

FIG 93 Small cross stitch

LONG CROSS STITCH

A long cross is worked across one thread and up over two, on alternate intersections of the canvas. The stitches of the next row fit in between those of the first, in a brickwork effect. Small in-filling stitches are necessary at the edge. It may also be worked diagonally as shown.

FIG 94 Long cross stitch

TIED CROSS STITCH

A long cross stitch is worked over three horizontal bars, and a small cross stitch ties it down at the centre. Alternatively it may be worked over two horizontal bars, with a straight stitch tying it down at the centre.

FIG 95 Tied cross stitch

RHODES STITCH

Long straight stitches are worked rotating around a square. The first stitch is worked from lower left to top right and after that the needle comes up to the right and goes down to the left of the previous stitch. When the square is filled, a short stitch is made over the centre.

FIG 96 Rhodes stitch

SATIN STITCH

Satin stitch can be worked in lines passing over two or more intersections of the canvas. It can also be worked in squares or other shapes.

FIG 97 Satin stitch

BACK STITCH

A stitch is made over one intersection and the needle is brought out at the next hole in front of this stitch. Each stitch is then made by taking the needle back into the same hole and out again two stitch lengths in front.

FIG 98 Back stitch

SMALL DIAGONAL STITCH

A diagonal stitch is worked over one intersection followed by a stitch over two intersections. This sequence is repeated. Subsequent rows fit in the gaps – the short stitch in line with the long, and vice versa.

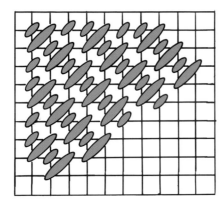

FIG 99 Small diagonal stitch

BRICK STITCH

This is worked in lines of straight stitches over two or four bars, leaving one bar uncovered between each. Subsequent rows are worked in between, in a brickwork effect. The first and last rows need half stitches to fill in the gaps.

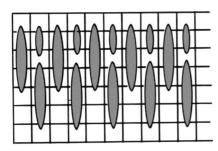

FIG 100 Brick stitch

MILANESE STITCH

Row 1: Work diagonal stitches over 1, 2, 3 and 4 bars of the canvas. The sequence is then repeated down across the required area.
Row 2: The same sequence is worked making blocks which fit in between those of the previous row, the stitch over 1 bar being placed in line with the one over 4 bars in the first row. Repeat these two rows to cover the required

FIG 101 Milanese stitch

area, making part stitches where necessary to fill in any gaps at the edges.

EDGING STITCHES

OVERCASTING

This is simpler to work than the edge stitch given below, and could be used instead if preferred. You may need double cotton or wool (yarn) for this.

Always bring the needle up from the back of the work and take it over the edge to make the next stitch. Start by making two stitches in the first hole. Work three stitches into the corners to give a good cover.

FIG 102 Overcasting

EDGE STITCH FOR PLASTIC CANVAS

This stitch is used for joining sections together, or for covering an edge. It has an interesting

FIG 103 Edge stitch for plastic canvas

FIG 104 Edge stitch for cotton canvas

plaited effect, which shows best if worked from the wrong side. Work at a tight tension, except when joining a lid to a box.

Although this stitch may look complicated it is actually just two movements – forward three bars and back two, repeated. Extra stitches are needed at the beginning and end to fill in properly.

1) Bring the needle up in the first hole, take it over the edge and come out at 2, two bars forward.
2) Take it back over the edge and out two bars back, in the first hole again.

Continue as follows:

3) Take it over the edge, and out three bars forward.
4) Take it over the edge and out two bars back.

Repeat 3 and 4 along the edge until the needle comes up in the last hole. Take it back over the edge and out one bar back, and bring it up in the last hole again. Fasten off securely. At a corner work three stitches into the corner hole, and continue along the next side.

EDGE STITCH FOR COTTON CANVAS

This is worked in a similar way, going forward six threads and back four all along the edge.

Fold the turning to the wrong side between the first and second threads next to the embroidery. One thread should show on the right side, and the holes should match up.

1) Bring the needle up in the first hole, take it over the edge and come out two threads forward.
2) Take it over the edge and out in the first hole again.
3) Take it over the edge and out four threads forward.
4) Take it over the edge and out in the first hole again.

Continue as follows:

5) Take the needle over the edge and out six threads forward.
6) Take it over the edge and out four threads back.

Repeat steps 5 and 6 until the needle comes up in the corner hole. Next go back four threads and up in the corner hole, back two threads and up in the corner again. Work three stitches into the corner hole and continue as before.

SURFACE EMBROIDERY STITCHES

STEM STITCH

Worked from left to right. Bring the needle up at the beginning of the line to be covered. Take it down to the right and up again a little to the left, keeping the thread below the needle. The lengths of the stitches may be varied, as may the slant.

FIG 105 Stem stitch

RAISED CHAIN BAND

A ladder of stitches is worked first and then chain stitches, which do not pass through the fabric, are worked over them.

Hold the work in a vertical position and bring the needle up at 1, centrally above the first ladder stitch. With the thread to the right, take the needle over and under the first bar. Now with the thread to the left, work a chain stitch over the same bar. Repeat this process to cover the ladder.

FIG 106 Raised chain band

SEEDING

Small stitches are worked at random, to give a powdered background.

FRENCH KNOTS

If worked correctly a pretty rose bud shape is achieved. The secret of success lies in keeping the thread taut against the fabric when pulling through to the back.

Bring the needle up to the right side and hold the thread in your left hand close to the fabric. Wrap the needle round it once or twice and, keeping the thread taut, insert the point into the fabric close to where it came out. Slide the knot down against the fabric, hold it under your

FIG 108 French knots

thumb and feed the thread gently through, only taking your thumb away at the last moment.

HERRINGBONE STITCH

As an embroidery stitch this is worked moving from left to right between parallel lines, taking a small back stitch alternately on each one. It is also used for lacing two turnings together when lining a box or mounting embroidery.

FIG 109 Herringbone

PULLED-WORK STITCHES

These stitches are worked at a tight tension, so that holes form in the fabric, giving an interesting contrast in texture. They may be worked freely on any loose weave fabric, as in the Pin Box in Chapter 2 and the pictures in Chapter 9, or on evenweave fabric to give a formal effect as in the needlecase and pincushion in Chapter 2.

FREELY-WORKED EYELETS

Straight stitches are worked into a central hole and pulled so that a hole forms at the centre.

FIG 110 Free eyelets

FIG 107 Seeding

The looser the weave, and the tighter the stitches are pulled, the bigger the hole.

EYELET STITCH

This consists of counted straight stitches worked into a central hole. Worked at a tight tension they give an interesting variation in texture.

FIG 111 Eyelet

FOUR-SIDED STITCH

This may be worked over two, three or four threads. All stitches on the back of the work are diagonal, which enables a good pull on the fabric to be achieved. Work from right to left, following the diagram. At the corner, take the needle down to complete the last stitch, turn the work and bring the needle up in position 3, continuing along the edge as before.

If this is used as a filling stitch, stitch 3-4 will double up with the stitches on the previous row.

FOUR-SIDED EDGE STITCH OR PICOT EDGING

At least ¾in (20mm) turnings are needed for this stitch. The examples here are worked over four threads. This could be varied to two or three if preferred.

Decide where your finished edge should be. Pull out a thread on this line (A), and then another, four threads inside it (B). The stitch is worked in two journeys. A tight tension on the horizontal stitches will give good picots to the finished edge. Work from right to left.

Row 1: Repeat the two stitches across the row, following the diagram. At the corners turn the work and continue as before (C). Pull out a thread four threads outside the stitching.

Row 2: Fold the fabric along the horizontal stitching along one side and finger press, lining up the withdrawn threads on front and back. These horizontal stitches will form the picot edge.

Complete the lower edge of the four-sided stitch as shown. Stitches 1-2 will go over the edge and out at 3, doubling up with stitch 1-2 of row 1.

Before working the last stitch on each side, trim the turning to the stitching. Fold the next side turning along the horizontal stitching as before, turn and continue, working double stitches over the corner for strength. Complete the edge in this way.

FIG 113 Four-sided edge stitch

FIG 112 Four-sided stitch

Thread Conversion Chart

Anchor	DMC	Anchor	DMC	Anchor	DMC	Anchor	DMC
19	347	160	813	352	300	846	936
20	816	161	826	358	433	856	3011
41	892	214	368	360	898	859	523
68	3687	216	367	372	738	860	3363
73	3689	218	890	373	3045	876	503
75	3354	259	772	376	842	879	500
76	3731	265	989	381	938	891	676
77	3350	268	3345	382	3371	893	225
89	917	293	727	386	746	895	223
95	554	300	3078	387	ecru	896	3721
98	553	302	743	388	3782	921	931
108	211	303	742	398	415	926	822
118	793	305	725	400	317	4146	754
127	939	307	783	843	3012	9575	758

Acknowledgements

I would like to thank Vivienne Wells for asking me to write this book. I would also like to thank all my friends for their help, encouragement and infinite patience in helping to work the embroidered samples. These include: Eileen Ellis, Hilary Harrison, Pauline Newland, Wendy Newland, Nancy Perrin, Sheila Tompkins, and all the members of my crafts class, who dropped what they were doing, and worked with a will.

Special thanks to Judith Casy for a heroic effort editing my manuscript, and to my husband for taming the word processor, doing the technical drawings, doing the cooking and tolerating a 5am alarm for many weeks.

Useful Addresses

UK

Meg Evans
29 New Road
Welwyn
Herts
AL6 0AQ
(Mail order, for most items listed in the projects, including Paterna in 4oz hanks)

Shades at Mace and Nairn
89 Crane Street
Salisbury
Wiltshire
SP1 2PY
(Mail order for a very wide range of supplies including some beads)

Coats Patons Crafts
PO Box 1
McMullen Road
Darlington
Co Durham
DL1 1YQ

DMC Creative World
Pullman Road
Wigston
Leicestershire
LE8 2DY

The Craft Collection
PO Box 1
Ossett
West Yorkshire
WF5 9SA
(Information on Paterna stockists)

Craft Creations Ltd
Units 1-7, Harpers Yard
Ruskin Road
Tottenham
London
N17 8NE
(Greetings cards and lining card)

Framecraft Miniatures Ltd
148-150 High Street
Aston
Birmingham
B6 4US
(Picture frames, brooches and porcelain boxes)

USA

Coats & Clark Inc
30 Patewood Drive
Suite 351
Greenville sc 29615

DMC Corporation
Port Keamy
Building 10
South Keamy
NJ 07032

Schrocks Crafts
1527 East Amherst Road
Massillon
Ohio 44646
(Mail order)

Needlecraft Shop
103 North Pearl Street
Big Sandy
Texas 75755
(Mail order)

Australia

Coats Patons Crafts
89-91 Peters Avenue
Mulgrave
Victoria 3170

DMC Needlecraft Pty Ltd
PO Box 317
Earlswood
NSW 2206